Also from Westphalia Press
westphaliapress.org

The Idea of the Digital University

Dialogue in the Roman-Greco World

The History of Photography

International or Local Ownership?: Security Sector Development in Post-Independent Kosovo

Lankes, His Woodcut Bookplates

Opportunity and Horatio Alger

The Role of Theory in Policy Analysis

The Little Confectioner

Non-Profit Organizations and Disaster

The Idea of Neoliberalism: The Emperor Has Threadbare Contemporary Clothes

Social Satire and the Modern Novel

Ukraine vs. Russia: Revolution, Democracy and War: Selected Articles and Blogs, 2010-2016

James Martineau and Rebuilding Theology

A Strategy for Implementing the Reconciliation Process

Issues in Maritime Cyber Security

A Different Dimension: Reflections on the History of Transpersonal Thought

Iran: Who Is Really In Charge?

Contracting, Logistics, Reverse Logistics: The Project, Program and Portfolio Approach

Unworkable Conservatism: Small Government, Freemarkets, and Impracticality

Springfield: The Novel

Lariats and Lassos

Ongoing Issues in Georgian Policy and Public Administration

Growing Inequality: Bridging Complex Systems, Population Health and Health Disparities

Designing, Adapting, Strategizing in Online Education

Pacific Hurtgen: The American Army in Northern Luzon, 1945

Natural Gas as an Instrument of Russian State Power

New Frontiers in Criminology

Feeding the Global South

Beijing Express: How to Understand New China

The Rise of the Book Plate: An Exemplative of the Art

The Handbook of Conundrums

by Edith B. Ordway

WESTPHALIA PRESS
An Imprint of Policy Studies Organization

The Handbook of Conundrums
All Rights Reserved © 2018 by Policy Studies Organization

Westphalia Press
An imprint of Policy Studies Organization
1527 New Hampshire Ave. NW
Washington, D.C. 20036
info@ipsonet.org

ISBN-13: 978-1-63391-671-5
ISBN-10: 1-63391-671-5

Cover design by Jeffrey Barnes:
jbarnesbook.design

Daniel Gutierrez-Sandoval, Executive Director
PSO and Westphalia Press

Updated material and comments on this edition
can be found at the Westphalia Press website:
www.westphaliapress.org

THE HANDBOOK OF CONUNDRUMS

THE HANDBOOK OF CONUNDRUMS

BY

EDITH B. ORDWAY
AUTHOR OF "THE ETIQUETTE OF TO-DAY," AND
"SYNONYMS AND ANTONYMS."

NEW YORK
GEORGE SULLY AND COMPANY

COPYRIGHT, 1914, BY
SULLY and KLEINTEICH
COPYRIGHT, 1915, BY
SULLY and KLEINTEICH

All rights reserved

PRINTED IN U. S. A.

PREFACE

This book presents a grindstone whereon the reader may whet his wits. It is of sufficient hardness to resist the coarsest metal of broad-bladed humor, and of sufficient fineness of grain to edge the best steel of fancy.

Like all grindstones, though its form is new, its ingredients are of remote origin. It has whetted many English and American blades for the battle of ideas, and is, therefore, in places, somewhat worn. There is, however, much absolutely fresh surface.

Any blade of fine temper properly ground upon it is warranted to cleave to the dividing asunder of such subtle distinctions as that between humorsome stupidity and precise wit, and that between the wit of laughter only and the wit of insight.

E. B. O.

INTRODUCTION

A CONUNDRUM is a riddle in the form of a question, the answer to which involves a pun. Originally the term was applied to any quaint expression. It is thus, in its modern form, a union of the elaborated riddle and the impromptu pun.

With the earliest development of intelligence came the discovery of likeness and difference in things, and the search for analogy was carried out along both sensible and absurd lines, the latter drifting into a double analogy of thought and form, of which the conundrum is the logical product.

The literatures of all peoples contain the riddle, which might be witty or serious as impulse prompted. All bright and clever minds have seen the possibilities of the pun, and so common is it as an impromptu form of wit among keen people, so general the temptation to fall into it, that it is looked upon with disfavor, as a pitfall for thought, which often prevents it from finishing its course.

The conundrum has, however, an ancient and honorable lineage, and, while not often given its precise form in conversation or anecdote, is readily adapted to the permanent embodiment of those flashes of wit which enlighten and cheer.

The ability to guess and to propound riddles was held in high respect in early times. Men of great physical prowess were expected to guess riddles to prove their mental prowess, and many were the contests of this sort which were held. The stakes in these contests were very high,—often life or honor. In Norse mythology the prize of such a contest was once the daughter of the god Thor; in another the life of the giant Vafthrudnir was forfeit when he failed to win in competition with the god Odin.

So in the old English ballad of the Elfin-knight, a maiden saves herself from an evil spirit by successfully guessing his riddles. Among many primitive peoples the game of riddle-reading was played with opposing sides, each headed by a champion, and with bets staked on the outcome. Often in bal-

INTRODUCTION

lads and folklore the hero's escape from death and final triumph hinge upon the guessing of a riddle.

The Semitic people held in high regard the power to read riddles, and this power, as in the story of Solomon, blends with the higher intelligence which makes for wisdom.

Perhaps the most famous of Hebrew conundrums is that of Samson, the strong of intellect as of body, who, when he found the honey which the wild bees had placed in the carcass of a lion, read to the Philistines this riddle: "Out of the eater came forth meat, and out of the strong came forth sweetness."

Among the Greeks and Romans, as among earlier peoples, all forms of wit and play of word and fancy were tried and popular. D'Israeli, in his "Curiosities of Literature," records that "It is certain that Cicero was an inveterate punster; and he seems to have been more ready with them than with repartees."

The story of the famous riddle of the Sphinx comes down from Greek mythology. The city of Thebes was infested by a monster having the body of a lion and the upper part of a woman. She lay crouching upon a rock near a narrow pass which led to the city, and propounded to all travelers a riddle, allowing all who guessed to pass safely, but killing all who failed. The uniform failure of all who came, and their subsequent slaughter, made great lamentation in the city. Œdipus, the unacknowledged son of the King of Thebes, who had shortly before unknowingly killed his father, undertook to rid the city of the monster. He boldly confronted the Sphinx, who asked him the riddle, "What animal is it that in the morning goes on four feet, at noon on two, and in the evening upon three?" Œdipus replied, "Man, who in childhood creeps on hands and knees, in manhood walks erect, and in old age goes with the aid of a staff." * The Sphinx thereupon cast herself from the rock and perished, and the Thebans made Œdipus king.

There is one age-old riddle, still current in Brittany, Germany, and Gascony, about which the tradition hovers that Homer died with vexation at not being able to discover the answer. It is, "What we caught we

---

* See Gayley's "Classic Myths in English Literature and in Art" (Boston, Ginn and Company, 1911).

INTRODUCTION

threw away, what we could not catch we kept."

Early folklore riddles dealt with natural phenomena. With the Wolofs the riddle of the wind asks, "What flies forever and rests never?" The Teutonic form was, "What can go in the face of the sun, yet leave no shadow?" The Basutos of South Africa ask: "What is wingless and legless, yet flies fast and cannot be imprisoned?" and answer, "The voice."

The oldest English riddles extant are among the fragments found in "The Exeter Book." These date back to the eighth century and were written in Northumbria. While these are not conundrums in the modern sense, they are very elaborate studies of analogy, and contain some of the most imaginative of Anglo-Saxon poetry.

In the early half of the seventeeth century there were published several small books, which contain the sources of many of the conundrums of the present day. These books have been brought together by W. Carew Hazlitt, under the title "Shakespeare's Jest-Books" (London, 1864). The dates of these books are variously 1600,

1630, 1636, and 1639. The form is narrative, with occasional dialogue, and approaches that of the conundrum, and the wit though far from subtle is often effective. Though the names of the authors of some of these books are known, the authorship of others is in doubt. They were to a considerable extent not attributable to one man, but were the bright sayings of the day.

The first chapter of the present volume, entitled "Early English Wit," brings together, in modernized form, some of the brightest of these sayings. The strangest thing about such a collection is to discover of what antiquity some current conundrums are. That is notably true of one taken from "Demaundes Joyous," printed by Wynkyn de Worde in 1511, namely:

"*Demaund.* How many straws go to a goose's nest?

"*A.* None, for lack of feet.

Besides the puns which may be made within a language itself, through the variety of meanings of words and the similarity of sound in different words, there is a certain class of hybrid puns and conundrums which

INTRODUCTION xiii

is made by the interchange of languages. The following story illustrates this class: A newly appointed and bashful young curate was visiting a young ladies' school in his parish. The ordeal of facing so many blooming young misses was endured until, the class in Virgil having been found ill-prepared and the teacher having requested that the translation be made word for word, he was startled by the declaration made by a pretty young lady, "We kiss him in turn" (*Vicissim,* in turn), whereupon he ungallantly fled.

When Laud was Archbishop to Charles I, it is related that the Court Jester made the punning grace, "Great praise be to God and little Laud to the Devil," which resulted in his banishment by the Archbishop.

Shakespeare uses the conundrum with a masterly hand, ringing many changes upon it and producing many effects, both grave and gay. An example of the quizzical dialogue which has the wit of the conundrum as its basis, is found in "Twelfth Night," Act I., scene 5:

Clown. Good madonna, why mournest thou?
Olivia. Good fool, for my brother's death.

Clown. I think his soul is in hell, madonna.
Olivia. I know his soul is in heaven, fool.
Clown. The more fool, madonna, to mourn for your brother's soul being in heaven.

While the conundrum ranks as the formal literary representative of the spontaneous pun, the literature of wit is alive with the naked pun in its original state. Pope, Hood, Lamb, and Holmes are the names of some whose punning arraignments of puns and punsters make them at once judges and prisoners at the bar.

Theodore Hook is accredited with the original pun which is the basis of a common conundrum. He bragged that he could make a pun on any subject, and immediately a friend suggested that he make one on the King. "The King is no subject," was the prompt rejoinder.

The poems of Thomas Hood, the "king of punsters," abound in puns, and the sort of wit, subtle or broad, which may be expressed in puns. He was primarily a poet, and manipulated words in a masterly fashion, not letting them deflect his thought. An example of the inevitableness of his punning is found in the poem on "Sally

Brown": "They went and told the sexton, and the sexton toll'd the bell."

A friendly contest between Hook and Hood, as to which could make the best pun, resulted in a draw, the efforts of the two men being of equal merit, according to the friend who was called upon to decide.

Alexander Pope, although disapproving of the pun as a trifling form of wit, once challenged his hearers to suggest a word upon which he could not make a pun. The word "keelhauling," meaning to draw a man under a ship, was given by a woman present. "That, Madam," replied Pope, "is indeed putting a man under a hardship."

The incident is told of Charles Lamb that once when in Salisbury Cathedral the constable remarked to him that eight people had dined at the top of the spire; whereupon Lamb remarked that they must be "very sharp set."

The story is told that a man noted for his wit in puns was asked in regard to the writings of Thomas Carlyle if he did not like "to expatiate in such a field?" He replied, "No. I can't get over the stile (style)."

From the riddle or pun it is but a short

step to the conundrum, which takes the pun from its purely factitious setting and gives it a general application and a permanent form. It is, when rightly constructed, at once interesting and instructive, teaching as much by negative as by affirmative statement. It embodies the ever new analogies between dissimilar things, and with a language so fertile in idiom as the English aids in its mastery. Used in application to historical and geographical subjects it may serve to fix names and places definitely in memory, as well as facts which but for the humorous interest given to them would be dry and easily forgotten.

There is a certain distinctive flavor to the current conundrums of a period which tells more of the popular interests of the time than anything but a newspaper could. The best conundrums of each period, or those that center around a great event, would make most illuminating historical reading. The opinions of the day are often more clearly expressed in a conundrum than in an essay. It would have been of interest to know what the wits, as well as the historians, said of Napoleon at Waterloo, of the Boston Tea Party, and of Washington and the Continental Congress. Possibly the opinion of posterity would not have differed so widely from that of the wits as from that of the contemporary chroniclers.

John Taylor, whose book, "Wit and Mirth," published in 1630, was one of the oldest and most distinctive original collections, was the forerunner of such punning poets as Hood and Holmes. In the dedication of his book, in order to forestall criticism for the publishing of sayings already well-known, he says: "Because I had many of them (the jests) by relation and heare-say, I am in doubt that some of them may be in print in some other Authors, which I doe assure you is more then I doe know." The authors of all compilations of conundrums in the almost three centuries since have had to make increasingly comprehensive acknowledgment, which the present author here hastens to give, having drawn from the great common sources, as well as from the unpublished current wit of the day.

CONTENTS

INTRODUCTION 7

CHAPTER	PAGE
I. EARLY ENGLISH WIT	1
II. MYTHOLOGICAL CONUNDRUMS . .	18
III. BIBLICAL CONUNDRUMS	20
IV. HISTORICAL CONUNDRUMS . . .	30
V. CONUNDRUMS OF THE CIVIL WAR PERIOD	38
VI. GEOGRAPHICAL CONUNDRUMS . .	44
VII. LITERARY CONUNDRUMS	52
VIII. CONUNDRUMS OF THE ALPHABET .	60
IX. GENERAL CONUNDRUMS	73
X. CHARADES, STORIES, AND CONTESTS	183

CHAPTER I

EARLY ENGLISH WIT

IN the anecdotes, dry remarks, repartees, and posers of this chapter, the sayings of which were current from about 1600 on to the present day, is seen the growth of the modern form of conundrum, which is adhered to largely in the remaining chapters of this book.

A poet was asked where his wits were. "A-wool-gathering," he answered. "No people have more need of it," was the reply.

A good client is like a study gown, which sits in the cold himself to keep his lawyer warm.

"Why do lawyers' clerks write such wide lines?" "It is done to keep the peace. For if the plaintiff should be in one line and the defendant in the next, with the lines too near together, they might perhaps fall together by the ears."

A master spoke in a strain which his servant did not understand. The servant thereupon asked that his master might rather give him blows than such hard words.

What great scholar is this same Finis, because his name is to almost every book?*

A prodigal is like a brush that spends itself to make others go handsome in their clothes.

An antiquary loves everything for being moldy and worm-eaten,—as Dutchmen do cheese.

It was said that a player had "an idle employment of it." "You are mistaken," was the reply, "for his whole life is nothing else but action."

A simple fellow in gay clothes was likened to a cinnamon tree,—because the bark was of more worth than the body.

---

*Hazlitt considers this witticism, found in "Conceits, Clinches, Flashes, and Whimzies" (London, 1639), the earliest of its kind, and calls attention to the discussion as to whether Shakespeare's plays were written by *Mr. Preface* or *Mr. Finis*.

One asked a favor of a prisoner, saying that he had hitherto found him a fast friend, and hoped he should find him so still.

A scholar who was much given to going abroad, was advised that he put away his cushion, as he would then "sit harder to his study."

It was remarked that "poetry and plain dealing were a couple of handsome wenches." It was replied that "he who weds himself to either of them shall die a beggar."

Why are women so crooked and perverse in their conditions? Because the first woman was made of a crooked thing.

One was advised to marry a little woman, because "of evils the least was to be chosen."

A rich lawyer, whose fortune had been made by the practice of his profession, desired to bequeath a certain sum to the insane asylum of Bedlam. Being questioned why, he replied that he had got his money of mad men, and he would give it to them again.

The trade of tooth drawer is a conscienceless one, because it is "nothing else but to take away those things whereby every man gets his living."

"A vainglorious man" was bragging that his father and uncle had founded a certain hospital. One answered, "'Tis true, but yet know that your father and your uncle were the mere confounders (co-founders) of that hospital you speak of."

It was said that corn was a quarrelsome creature, because it rose by the blade, and fell by the ears with those that cut it.

A tailor was commended for his dexterity, whereupon it was remarked that tailors had their business at their fingers' ends.

Colliers and mine-workers, it was said, should be well acquainted with all the philosophical secrets of the earth, because they had a deeper knowledge of it than any others.

"Of all knaves there's the greatest hope of a cobbler, for though he be never so idle a fellow, yet he is still mending."

"A smith," said one, "is the most pragmatical fellow under the sun, for he hath always many irons in the fire."

HANDBOOK OF CONUNDRUMS

The proverb, "Wit bought is better than wit taught," had added to it the comment, "because he that never bought any is but a natural wit," embodying the play on the word "natural," the early name for "fool."

Tall men are the most happy, because they are nearer heaven than other men. They should also be great politicians, because they have extraordinary reach.

Of all soldiers musketeers are the most lazy, for they are always at rest.

It is necessary that some rich men be dunces, because pretenders to learning may get preferment, and good wits will be able to help themselves.

Carpenters are the most civil men because they never do their business without a rule.

A hangman is the most trusty of friends, for, if he once have to do with a man, he will see him hanged before he shall want money or anything else.

Physicians have the best of it. If they do well, the world proclaims it; if ill, the earth covers it.

A man and his wife were fighting. One

was asked why he did not part them, and replied, that he "had been better bred than to part man and wife."

Tobacconists (users of tobacco) would endure war well, for they would never be stifled with fire and smoke.

Fiddlers are very unfortunate in their calling, for they never do anything but it is against the hair (fiddlestring).

Smiths are the most irregular of handicrafts men, because they never think that they are better employed than when they are addicted to their vices.

It is no great matter what a drunkard says in his drink, for he never says anything that he can stand to.

"Horse-keepers and ostlers (let the world go which way it will, though there be never so much alteration in times and persons) are still stable men."

A hypocrite is odious to God, to man, and to the devil. God hates him, because he is not what he seems; man hates him, because he seems what he is not; and the devil hates him, because he seems not what he truly is.

Stage players are the most philosophical of men, because they are as content in rags as in robes.

"Roaring gallants" are like peddlers,— they carry their whole estate upon their backs.

An occulist is an excellent sleight-of-hand performer; because if he undertakes to cure a blind man, he will so do it that the patient shall see he does it.

He that buys a horse in Smithfield and does not look upon him before he buy him, with a pair of spectacles, makes his horse and himself a pair of sorrowful spectacles for others to look on.

Cobblers must be good men because they set men upright, and are always employed in mending soles.

A wild young gentleman desired to sell his land, and was asked the reason, to which he answered that he hoped to go to heaven, but could not possibly do so until he had forsaken earth.

A drunkard, returning home at night, found his wife hard at her spinning. She reproved him for his ill husbandry, and commended herself for her good housewifery. He replied that she had no great cause to chide, for, as she had been spinning, he came all the way home reeling.

An ignorant drunken surgeon, who killed all patients that came under his hands, boasted that he was a better man than the parson; "For," he said, "your cure maintains but yourself, but my cures maintain all the sextons in the town."

A man by the name of Stone fell off his horse into deep water, from which he struggled, but not without some danger. His companion laughed, and when rebuked, replied that any man would laugh to see a stone swim.

One who had received a threat that another would break his head with a stone, replied, "It is a hard matter to break my head with a stone."

A physician sought to collect a bill due for service to a patient who had died. He was told that it was a work of charity to visit the sick, but if he wanted money so badly the only way was for him to visit the dead, and then he would not want money any more.

The following dialogue took place between two friends: "I love to hear a man talk nonsense." "I know you love to hear yourself talk as well as any man."

A gentleman made some purchases upon trust in a shop, promising the proprietor that he would owe him so much money. The proprietor was for a time content, but when he sought to collect the payment, the gentleman told him that he had not promised to pay him, but had promised to owe him so much money, and that he would not break his promise, as he would have to if he paid the debt.

"What are Shakespeare's works worth, all bound together?" "Not a farthing." "Not worth a farthing? How so?" "His plays are worth a great deal of money, but I never heard that his works are worth anything at all."

A man met his friend riding without boots, and asked him about what business he went. The friend replied that it was a matter of great importance, and that he was in great haste. The man said, "I am afraid that your labor is lost." "Why?" inquired the rider. "Because," was the reply, "you ride of a bootless errand."

Which of the letters of the alphabet are the most authentic on a bill or bond? I O U.

Why do not men and their wives agree better nowadays? Because men are now more learned, and know that "it is false concord that the masculine and feminine gender should agree at all."

A man had the pictures of the five senses stolen from his house, and came to a justice, desiring that the thieves might be bound to the peace. "For what?" asked the justice. "For stealing your pictures?" "Yes," replied the man. "I thought," said the justice, "that you had lost your senses, that you talk so idly."

One in the midst of a crowd of people on the top of the steeple of St. Paul's Church, London, had his pocket picked. "What villains are these," he exclaimed, "to pick a man's pocket in church!" "Nay, sir," said another, "you are but robbed upon the highway."

A scholar was fond of sitting in a study

hung around with brown paper, because, he would say, he did sometimes love to sit in a brown study.

"Why are there drums in the wars?" "To stir up the valor of the soldiers." "Strange, for wheresoever the victory falls, the drums are sure to be beaten."

Why does B stand before C? Because a man must B before he can C.

How long is the longest letter in the English alphabet? An L long.

Two men, of whom one was a goldsmith, conspired together to steal a silver bowl. When they had procured it, the goldsmith gilded it over that it might not be known. They were arrested, however, and when the matter came to trial, the judge said, that though the other stole it, yet the guilt of the fact lay upon the goldsmith.

One came upon a sexton making a grave for a great tall fellow by the name of Button, and asked him for whom that extraordinarily long grave was. The sexton answered, that he had made many longer than that, and said it was but a button-hole compared with some graves that he had made.

A man, whose name was You, married a woman of the same name, and was ever after called "Master W."

One was wondering why the people of Æthiopia did not write straight along as the northern people do, and another answered that they wrote under the line, and that was the reason of it.

A dyer, who was an idle drunken fellow, complained to a scholar that he had bad luck in his business, and that usually those things which he took to dye were spoiled. The scholar told him that the only way to have this amended was to reform himself, for he that lived ill could never dye well.

What herb is there that cures all diseases? Thyme.

An upholsterer rebuked his apprentice because he was not nimble enough at his work, and had not his nails and hammer in readiness when he should use them; and said that when he himself was an apprentice he was taught to have his nails at his fingers' ends.

What does that young man deserve who loves always to be in a playhouse? A box.

One expressed surprise that there were so many pickpockets about the streets, notwithstanding that there was a watch at every corner. It was answered that this was all one, for a pickpocket would as gladly meet with a watch as with anything else.

One who was skilled in writing shorthand offered to teach a lawyer's clerk his skill, but the latter thanked him for his offer, and told him that they could not live by making short hand of anything.

A coward related to his friend that one had given him a box upon the ear, but that he, instead of returning the blow, had turned to him the other ear also. The friend replied, "Sure, there was a great fight betwixt you, when blows were given on both sides."

The word Interpreter is derived from Inter-prater, for one that prated betwixt two that spoke several languages.

A company of gentlemen entered a tavern whose sign was the Moon, and called for a quart of sack. The drawer told them that they had none, and that the man in the Moon always drank claret.

A countryman, being asked how a certain

river which ran through that country was called, replied, that they never had need to call the river, for it came without calling.

A country fellow who was unaccustomed to paved streets, came to London, and a dog suddenly ran out of one of the houses and came furiously at him. The fellow stooped to pick up a stone to throw at the dog, but finding them all fast rammed or paved into the ground, exclaimed, "What a strange country am I in, where the people tie up the stones, and let the dogs loose!"

A justice of the peace, angry with a pilfering knave, said, "Sirrah, if thou dost not mend thy manner, thou wilt be shortly hanged, or else I will be hanged for thee." The bold knave replied, "I thank your worship for that kind offer, and I beseech your worship not to be out of the way, when I shall have occasion to use you."

A sailor riding from Dover to London on a tired horse, was urged by his companions to ride faster. "I can come no faster," he replied. "Do you not see that I am becalmed?"

Between twelve and one o'clock one asked

me what o'clock it was. I answered, "Little or nothing." He demanded what I meant. I replied that, it being not one of the clock, it was to be reckoned or counted for naught, as that which is less than one is little or nothing.

(James the First and his successor created knights profusely for the purpose of raising money. From this fact grew the following conundrum:) Why did a knight take place of a gentleman? Because they were knights nowadays before they were gentlemen.

Why do fat men love their ease so much? Because the soul in a fat body lies soft, and is therefore loath to rise.

Who is he that has a fine wit in jest? A fool in earnest.

One, hearing that a traveler had been on the peak of Teneriffe (which is supposed to be one of the highest hills in the world), asked him why he had not stayed there, for he was sure he would never come so near heaven again.

What countryman is the devil? A Spaniard; for Spaniards, like the devil, trouble the whole world. (1600.)

Musicians may be compared to chameleons, because they live by air.

What countryman is a ploughman? They are all born in Hungary.

Printers are the most lawless men in the kingdom, because they commit faults with license.

Why should men think there is a world in the moon? Because they are lunatic. (This refers to the book, "A Discovery of a New World," by Bishop Wilkins, which had just appeared in 1638.)

It was asked of one who wore a threadbare coat, whether his coat were not sleepy. "Why do you ask?" queried the owner. "Because," was the reply, "I think it hath not had a nap this seven year."

One remarked "that it was a good fashion that was worn nowadays" (1639), "because the tailors had so contrived that there was little or no waste in a whole suit."

The philosopher's stone had need turn all metals to gold because the study of it turns all a man's gold to other metal.

"A Gallant with a galloping wit was

mounted upon a running horse toward a town named Tame, within ten miles of Oxford, and, riding at full speed, he met an old man, and asked him, 'Sirrah, is this the way to Tame?' 'Yes, sir,' he replied, 'your horse, I'll warrant you, if he were as wild as the devil.'

"This is a riddle to a fool, methinks,
  And seems to want an Œdipus or Sphinx,
But, Reader, in my book I hold it fit*
  To find you lines, yourself must find you wit."

---
*Sufficient.

CHAPTER II

MYTHOLOGICAL CONUNDRUMS

Where was Time raised? In the lapse of ages.

How do we know that Jupiter wore very pinching boots? Because we read of his struggles with the tight-uns (Titans).

What great astronomer is like Venus's chariot? Her-shell (Herschell).

Why does a woman residing up a pair of stairs remind you of a goddess? Because she's a second floorer (Flora).

Why is a man looking for the philosopher's stone like Neptune? Because he's a sea-king (a-seeking) what never was.

If all the seas were dried up, what would Neptune say? I really haven't an ocean (a notion).

If a young lady were to wish her father to pull her on the river, what classical name might she mention? You row, pa (Europa).

Why is Orpheus always in bad company? Because you never see him without a lyre.

If the Greeks had pushed Pan into the Bay of Salamis, what would he have been when he came out? A dripping Pan.

What did Io die of? Io-dide of potassium.

When does a lady think her husband a Hercules? When he can't get on without his club.

What girl does Echo think can best answer questions? Ann, sir.

Why was Leander voluntarily drowned? It was through his-whim (his swim) only.

Why is a coach going down a steep hill like St. George? Because it is always drawn with the drag-on.

CHAPTER III

BIBLICAL CONUNDRUMS

What three words did Adam use when he introduced himself to Eve, which read backwards and forwards the same? "Madam, I'm Adam."

At what time of day was Adam born? A little before Eve.

Why was the first day of Adam's life the longest? Because it had no Eve.

How were Adam and Eve prevented from gambling? Their pair o' dice (Paradise) was taken away from them.

What stone should have been placed at the gate of Eden after the expulsion? Adamantine (Adam ain't in).

Why did Adam bite the apple Eve gave him? Because he had no knife.

At what time was Adam married? Upon his wedding Eve.

What evidence have we that Adam used sugar? Because he raised Cain.

Who was the first man condemned to hard labor for life? Adam.

Who was first interested in horse racing? Adam—he was the father of the race.

How many apples were eaten in the Garden of Eden? Eve ate, and Adam, too, and the devil won,—eleven in all.

What one word will name the common parent of both beasts and man? A-dam.

What was the first surgical operation performed without the aid of instruments? The extraction of a rib of Adam to be made into a wife.

Why ought Adam to have been perfectly satisfied with his wife? Because she was cut out especially for him.

How did Adam and Eve feel when they left the Garden of Eden? Put out.

Why were the gates of Eden shut after Adam and Eve went out? To keep the dam(p) air out.

What fur did Adam and Eve wear? Bear (bare) skin.

Why had Eve no fear of the measles? Because she'd Adam (had 'em).

For what was Eve made? For Adam's Express Company.

What did Adam first plant in the Garden of Eden? His foot.

Who first introduced walking-sticks? Eve gave Adam a little Cain.

What kind of cottages did Adam's sons prefer? Cottages with eaves (Eves).

Was our mother Eve High or Low Church? Adam thought her Eve-angelical.

What did Adam and Eve do when they got out of Eden? Raised Cain.

Why was Paradise like a cucumber? Because it had a pair-in (paring).

When was the first gambling? When Adam and Eve cast up a Paradise (pair o' dice) for an apple.

When did fruit first begin to swear? When the apple damned the first pair.

Who was the fastest runner in the world? Adam—he was first in the human race.

How long did Cain hate his brother? As long as he was able (Abel).

Why was Cain's murder like the main strength of his leg? Because it was a sin-new.

How can a whipping be ordered for a boy in five Old Testament names? Adam, Seth, Eve, Cain, Abel.

Why is a printing press like the forbidden fruit? Because from it springs a knowledge of good and evil.

What was four weeks old when Cain was born, and is not yet five? The moon.

Who first introduced salt pork into the Navy? Noah, when he took Ham into the ark.

Why was Noah obliged to stoop on entering the ark? Because, although the ark was high, Noah was a higher ark (Hierarch).

In what place did the cock crow so loud that all the world heard him? In the ark.

Which animal took most luggage into the ark, and which the least? The elephant, who had his trunk; while the fox and the cock had only a brush and a comb between them.

Who was the greatest financier of early times? Noah,—he floated his stock when all the world was in liquidation.

Where did Noah strike the first nail in the ark? On the head.

What was Noah busy about in the ark? Preserving pairs.

Where did Noah keep his bees? In the Archives.

How do we know that Noah had beer in the ark? Because the kangaroo went in with hops, and the bear was always *Bruin*.

What did the cat say when she looked out of the window of the ark? Is that Ararat?

In what order did Noah come from the ark? He came forth.

When did Abraham sleep five in a bed? When he slept with his forefathers.

Why did Joseph's brethren put him in the pit? They thought that it was a good opening for the young man.

Where is the theater mentioned in the Bible? Where Joseph left the family circle and went into the pit.

Who had the first free entrance into a

theater? Joseph, when he got into the pit for nothing.

What person in the Bible died a death that no one else ever died—and a part of whose shroud is on every dining table? Lot's wife.

What did Lot do when his wife turned to salt? Got a fresh one.

What scene in the life of Moses, the law-giver, reminds us of a gladiatorial show at Rome? The bulrushes.

Why was Moses the wickedest man that ever lived? Because he broke all the Ten Commandments at once.

Where are bank checks mentioned in the Bible? Pharaoh got a check on the bank of the Red Sea—crossed by Moses and Co.

Why was Pharaoh's daughter like a broker? Because she drew a little prophet from the rushes on the bank.

What was Pharaoh's chief objection to Moses? He found him more plague than prophet.

How do we know that there was a panic in the early days of Moses? Because there were rushes on the banks of the Nile, and Pharaoh's daughter withdrew a valuable deposit.

Why do we assume that Moses wore a wig? Because sometimes he was seen with Aaron (hair on), and sometimes without.

If you were to throw a white stone into the Red Sea, what would it become? Wet.

Who were the first mathematicians mentioned in the Bible? The Children of Israel, who multiplied upon the face of the earth.

What is the difference between the ancient Israelites and modern washstands? The former had hewers of wood and drawers of water; the latter have ewers of water and drawers of wood.

Why would it be impossible to starve in the desert of Sahara? Because of the sandwiches (sand which is) there.

How did the sandwiches get there? When Ham was sent there with his followers, who were bred (bread) and mustered (mustard), and when Lot's wife was turned into a pillar of salt, all but-ter (but her) went into the desert.

Who was the oldest man that ever lived, yet who died before his father did? Methuselah: his father Enoch did not die, but was translated.

If Richard Jones were milking a cow too quickly, what ancient name would that animal mention? Melchisedek (Milk easy, Dick).

What man had no father? Joshua, the son of Nun.

Who took the first newspapers? Cain took A-Bell's Life, and Joshua countermanded the Sun.

Why was the giant Goliath very much astonished when David hit him with a stone? Because such a thing had never entered his head before.

How many soft-boiled eggs could the giant Goliath eat upon an empty stomach? One, after which his stomach was not empty.

What ancient king was often literally in his contemporaries' mouth? Agag.

What is the difference between Solomon and Rothschild? The one was king of the Jews, the other Jew of the kings.

Where did the Witch of Endor live—and end-her days? At Endor.

Who was hanged for not wearing a wig? Absalom.

In what tongue did Balaam's donkey speak? Probably in he-bray-ic.

Why would Samson have made an excellent actor? Because he could so easily bring down the house.

Why is the glass I drank out of yesterday like Nebuchadnezzar in his debased condition? Because it was my tumbler (might humbler).

What is the difference between Nineveh and a donkey-boy? One is in Assyria, the other is an ass-hurryer.

Who was the first unfortunate speculator? Jonah, because he got taken in.

What did the whale gain in the little transaction between him and Jonah? The whale got all the prophet.

Why was the whale which swallowed Jonah like a milkman who has retired on an independence? Because he took a great profit (prophet) out of the water.

How did Jonah feel when the whale was going to swallow him? Down in the mouth—as if he was going to blubber.

What divine law did the whale obey when he swallowed Jonah? Jonah was a stranger and he took him in.

Who was Jonah's tutor? The whale that brought him up.

Wherein did the prophet Jonah differ from the modern theologians? Because while he disagreed with the whale, they disagree about him.

Why was John the Baptist like a penny? Because he was one cent (sent).

Who won the first horse race in the Bible? Herodias' daughter when she got a head of John the Baptist on a charger.

When is a policeman like the good Samaritan? When he comes out of some area (Samaria).

Which are the two smallest things mentioned in the Scripture? The widow's mite, and the wicked flee.

Why is a good wife like the devil? While the husbandman sleepeth, she seweth (soweth) tears (tares).

CHAPTER IV

HISTORICAL CONUNDRUMS

There has been but one king crowned in England since the conquest. What king was he? James I. He was King of Scotland before he was King of England.

When Louis Philippe was deposed, why did he lose less than any of his subjects? Because, while he lost only a crown, they lost a sovereign.

Why is a portrait of Queen Elizabeth like a wager which is neither lost nor won? Because it is a drawn Bet.

What Egyptian official would a little boy mention if he were to call his mother to the window to see something wonderful? "Mammy, look!" (Mameluke).

What young ladies won the battle of Salamis? The Miss Tocles (Themistocles).

Who was the most wretched of all the

murderers of Julius Cæsar? The miserable Cinna (sinner).

What is the difference between the Emperor of Russia and a beggar? One issues manifestoes; the other manifests toes without 'is shoes.

Why is the Emperor of Russia like a greedy schoolboy on Christmas Day? Because he's confounded Hung(a)ry, and longs for Turkey.

Why is chloroform like Mendelssohn? Because it is one of the great composers of modern times.

Why was William Tell like a post? Because they couldn't get a bough out of him.

The name of what character in history would a person mention in asking the servant to put coal on the fire? Philip the Great (fill up the grate).

Why are volunteers like Lord Nelson? Because the last thing he did was to die for his country, and that is about the last thing the volunteers intend doing.

Why did the population of Rome decrease just before the fall of the empire? Because the Romans had ceased to practice husbandry.

When Charles I was beheaded, of what dish did the executioner dine, and where? He took a chop at the King's Head.

Why ought Charles I to have preferred burning to decapitation? Because a hot steak (stake) is always preferable to a cold chop.

Why did the Highlanders do most execution at Waterloo? Because every man had one kilt before the battle began.

Why are the Royal Academicians the greatest swells ever known? Because Solomon, even in all his glory, was not R. A.'d (arrayed) like one of these.

What piece of music did the Romans, at the time of the early Christians, most enjoy? A stab at martyr (A Stabat Mater).

If a nice plump Member of Parliament were eaten uncooked by savages, why would he be like Louis Napoleon? Because he would be served as an M. P. raw (emperor).

Why is the list of celebrated musical composers like a saucepan? Because it is incomplete without a Handel.

When was Napoleon I most shabbily dressed? When out at Elba (elbow).

What was once the most fashionable cap in Paris? The mob—without a crown.

In what respects were the governments of Algiers and Malta as different as light from darkness? The one was governed by deys, the other by knights.

Why is the Delaware River like an inkstand? Because Penn was the first man who entered it.

Why did Marcus Curtius leap into the gulf in Rome? Because he thought it a good opening for a young man.

What were the odds at the battle of Aliwal? They were six (Sikhs) and we (the English) one (won).

What Indian battle tried the metal (mettle) of the English soldiers? The battle of Assay(e).

Who is the first little boy mentioned by a single word in the history of England? Chap. I.

Who was the first postman? Cadmus. He carried letters from Phœnicia to Greece.

Where was Humboldt going when he was thirty-nine years old? Into his fortieth year.

What three letters give the name of a famous Roman general? C P O (Scipio).

Why did Louis Philippe omit to take his umbrella when he left Paris? Just as he left the rain (reign) was over.

Why are the English the worst judges of cattle in the world? Because the Pope sent them a bull and they thought it a bore (boar).

If you wish a very religious man to go to sleep, by what imperial name should you address him? Nap-holy-un (Napoleon).

Why is the palace of the Louvre the cheapest ever erected? Because it was built for one sovereign—and finished for another.

Why is it only natural that the memory of Guy Fawkes should be execrated? Because he was the inventor of parliamentary trains, and they are wretchedly slow.

Show that a simple typographical error

was the cause of the defeats of the poor Austrians (1866). They sent for reserves, and got reverses.

Why is a worn-out shoe like ancient Greece? Because it once had a Solon (sole on).

Why should Columbus be classed among astronomers rather than among explorers? Because he dicovered a whole New World.

What's the difference between a middle-aged cooper and a trooper of the Middle Ages? The one is used to put a head on his cask, the other used to put a cask (casque) on his head.

What fruit is like a Guy Fawkes? A fig, for is it not an F I G (effigy)?

How is it England and Russia conjointly govern the ocean? Because England rules the waves, and Russia the serfs.

What was the difference between Shakespeare and Queen Elizabeth? One was a *won*der, the other a *Tu*dor.

What Tory do the Whigs want on their side? Vic-tory.

It went before Queen Mary, it followed

King William to the end? The letter "m."

Who caught the fossil fishes? The geological fissures (fishers).

Why was the Shah of Persia, during his visit to England, the best card-player in the world? Because the swells gave up their clubs; workmen threw up their spades, and the ladies were within an ace of losing their hearts, when he came to show his diamonds.

Why was Martin Luther like a dyspeptic robin? The Diet of Wurms did not agree with him.

When was beef-tea introduced into England? When Henry VIII dissolved the Pope's bull.

Why could not Napoleon III insure his life? Because no man living was able to make out his policy.

What is the difference between two celebrated Saxon leaders of the fifth century and two others famous in these days? The former were Engist and Horsa, the latter are engines and horses.

What celebrated battle was fought in a dirty slum? The battle of A-gin-court.

What did Queen Elizabeth take her pills in? In cider (inside her).

What was Joan of Arc made of? Maid of Orleans.

What did they find under the Maine? A horse's neck.

What ought to be Sir Edwin Landseer's motto? Give a dog a good name and—hang him.

Some one mentioning that " columba " was the Latin for a " dove," it gave rise to the following: What is the difference between the Old World and the New? The former was discovered by *Columba,* who started from Noah; the latter by Columbus, who started from Ge-noa.

What is the difference between Kossuth and a half-starved countryman? One is a native of Hungary, the other is a hungry native.

Who may be said to have had the largest family in America? George Washington, for he was the father of his country.

CHAPTER V

Conundrums of the Civil War Period

Why does our army differ from the army of the Revolution? Because in one case the army is bound to defend Washington, in the other Washington was bound to defend the army.

Why is the Republican Party like a celebrated English ruler of the seventeenth century, "Oliver Cromwell, the Blacksmith"? Because it breaks asunder the chains of despotism and adds a link on (A. Lincoln) to history.

Why is an owl in the daylight like the President of the United States? Because he is a-blinkin' (Abe Lincoln).

Why is one of the new Treasury notes like a young lady's love letter? Because it is the acknowledgment of a loan made (lone maid) to which an unusual amount of interest is attached.

Why is the American Union a puzzle to the most profound astronomers? Because some of its " stars " have gone, and they cannot predict their return.

Why is General McClellan like the Established Church? Because he governs by Can(n)on Law.

Why is a diamond in a cup of cold water like the Union? Because it will not dissolve.

Why are the shot and shell of the blockading squadron like lovers' vows? Because they are intended for privateers (private ears).

Why are American greenbacks like the Jews? Because they are the product of Abraham, and no one knows if they will ever be redeemed.

Upon what guard do the New York Zouaves most desire to be put? Beaureguard.

Why would the colors of our national ensign make a good dress for ladies? Because they are colors that won't run.

Why are our fashionable ladies like a certain class of the city employees? Because they may be seen by scores on a fair day sweeping the streets.

In what relation does the President of the United States stand to Adam? As second son, because his name is Abe L. (Abel).

Why is it impossible for the government to grant the request of our Southern brethren? Because children in arms are never left alone.

Why, when the rebels smite us upon the right cheek, should we refuse to turn towards them the left cheek also? Because they have too much "cheek" already.

Why is Major General McClellan like Charles Dickens? Because he is the author of "Great Expectations."

Why are Jeff Davis's letters of marque like secrets? Because they are for privateers (private ears).

Why was Cain an enemy of President Lincoln? Because he hated Abe L.

Why is our army like an entry clerk? Because it is ready to charge.

Why is President Lincoln like a mariner on a desolate shore? Because he looks to Seward (seaward).

How does the Copyright Law affect the war? It gives us the right to *enter*, according to act of Congress, all the rebel States.

Why cannot rebels ever dress well? Because they have proved, by deserting their flag, that they have no eye for colors.

Why was the capture of Fort Hatteras like an English nobleman's mansion? Because there was a Butler engaged in it.

Why will Americans have more cause to remember the letter S than any other letter in the alphabet? Because it is the beginning of secession and the end of Jeff Davis.

Why should it not be loyal for a Union lady to accept a token of regard from a lover at the present time? Because it would be receiving a Beauregard (beau-regard).

Why is the rebellion like the world? Because it is coming to an end.

Why has Massachusetts done more towards the war loan than any other State? Because she has sent even her Banks.

Why are two lovers pledged to each other like the Federal Army before Washington? Because they have lately had an engagement and go in strong for the Union.

Why is a hen looking into a rotten pumpkin like the Southern Confederacy? Because she is trying to see seed (secede).

Why is the city of Washington like a despairing old maid? Because she has looked long and in vain for a Beauregard.

What one sentence expresses the wish of both the Southern Confederacy and the United States government? Let us alone (a loan).

What route should our army take at the present? The rout of the enemy.

Why is a man just knighted like a nutmeg? Because he's grated.

Why are lamps like the Thames? Because they have lighters.

Why is a sedan chair like the world? Because it's between two poles.

What is the most favorable season to have your letters from India? The season which brings the monsoon.

How do you know that the Queen approves of the penny postage? Because she gives her countenance to it.

Why is the old elm on Boston Common like the ladies of Boston? Because they are well hooped.

How long should a lady's crinoline be made? A little over two feet.

Why are ladies who wear large crinolines ugly? Because they are not even passable.

Why are washerwomen unreasonable? They expect soft water when it rains hard.

Why are they the greatest of coquettes? They wring men's ruffled bosoms.

CHAPTER VI

GEOGRAPHICAL CONUNDRUMS

What would happen if a colored waiter dropped a platter with a turkey upon it? The humiliation of Africa, the fall of Turkey, the destruction of China, and the overflowing of Greece.

What river is that which runs between two seas? The Thames—between Chel-sea and Batter-sea.

When is the river Thames good for the eyes? When it is high (eye) water.

Which are the lightest men—Scotchmen, Irishmen, or Englishmen? In Ireland there are men of Cork; in Scotland men of Ayr; but in England, on the Thames, there are lighter men.

What city of the world do artists make the most drawings of? Cork.

What islands would form a cheerful luncheon party? Friendly, Society, a Sandwich, and Madeira.

Which one of the United States is the largest and most popular? The state of matrimony.

Why is a young man engaged to a young lady like a man sailing for a port in France? Because he is bound to Havre (have her).

How many young ladies does it take to reach from New York to Philadelphia? About one hundred, because a Miss is as good as a mile.

Why is Great Britain like Palestine? Because it's the Holy Land (whole island).

If a man and his wife go to Europe together, what is the difference in their mode of traveling? He goes abroad, and she goes along.

Why are the Germans like quinine and gentian? Because they are two-tonics (Teutonics).

What is the most difficult river on which to get a boat? Arno, because there Arno boats there.

Why should we pity the young Esquimaux?

Because each one of them is born to blubber, —and ever to be-wail fishing, and walking with his snows frozen.

Why was the country of Phœnicia like an automobile? Because it had a Tyre on its border.

Why is the Empress of the French always in bad company? Because she is ever surrounded by Paris-ites.

What sea would a man like most to be in on a wet day? Adriatic (a dry attic).

How many Spanish noblemen does it take to make an Englishman run? Ten-dons.

What's the difference between an Irishman frozen to death and a Highlander on a mountain-peak in January? One is kilt with the cold, and the other cold with the kilt.

What county of England, if you dislike it extremely, would you run the chance of being stifled in? If you hate Suffolk, you would, very naturally, Suffolk-hate when in it (suffocate).

Two Spaniards went up in a balloon. The balloon burst. What nationality were they while coming down? The one came down a

Russian (a-rushing); the other caught on a telegraph wire and came down a Pole.

When is a tradesman at the seaside, though in London? When he comes from Dover to *Deal.*

How many cows' tails would it take to reach from Boston to New York? One, if it was long enough.

What is more foolish than sending coals to Newcastle? Sending milk to Cowes.

Why is the map of Turkey like a frying-pan? Because it has Greece (grease) at the bottom.

Why is the steeple of St. Paul's Church, London, like Ireland? Because there is a bell fast in it (Belfast).

What part of a bag of grain is like a Russian soldier? A coarse-sack (Cossack).

Why is a drunkard hesitating to sign the pledge like a skeptical Hindoo? Because he is in doubt whether to give up his jug or not (Juggernaut).

Why is a dissipated young man like Berlin, the capital of Germany? Because he is always on a Spree.

What nation is it which, when allied to us, becomes the very home of despair? Tartar-us.

Where ought children who bite their fingers to be sent? To gnaw-thumb-erland (Northumberland).

Why is a short man struggling to kiss a tall woman like an Irishman going up Vesuvius? Because, sure, he's trying to get at the mouth of the crater.

What is the greatest miracle ever worked in Ireland? Waking the dead.

Why is a Welshman like a beggar? Owing to the Menai Straits through which he goes.

For what reason ought a Frenchman who speaks imperfect English and an Englishman who is equally unacquainted with French never to converse together? To prevent their using bad language.

Why is Ireland likely to become rich? Because the capital is always Dublin (doubling).

What two letters make a county in Massachusetts? S X (Essex).

Why is the wick of a candle like Athens? It is in the midst of grease (Greece).

Why is China a desirable country for a man to select a wife in? Because he can make up his mind from pickin' to choose Ann (Pekin to Chusan).

What is the difference between the North and South Pole? All the difference in the world.

What part of Spain does your cat, sleeping by herself on the hearth-rug, resemble? Cat-alone-here (Catalonia).

Why is Westminster Abbey like a hearth? Because the ashes of the great (grate) lie there.

Why are corn and potatoes like Chinese idols? Because they have ears which cannot hear, and eyes which cannot see.

Which one of the Seven Wonders of the World are railway engines like? The coal-horses of roads (Colossus of Rhodes).

Why may we doubt the existence of the Giants' Causeway? There are so many sham-rocks in Ireland, this may be one of them.

What is the difference between a certain part of Africa and the shade of Hamlet's father stalking in winter? One is the Gold Coast, the other the cold ghost.

Why is love like the Erie Canal? It's an internal transport.

Why is New York City like a flash light? It has a Battery.

When is a tourist in Ireland like a donkey? When he is going to Bray.

Why is a nabob like a beggar? He is an India gent (indigent).

Why is wit like a Chinese lady's foot? Because brevity is the sole (soul) of it.

What is a man like who is in the middle of the Thames and can't swim? Like to be drowned.

Why is the Hudson River like a shoe? Because it is a great place for tows (toes).

Why is a pleasure trip to Egypt fit only for very old gentlemen? Because it is a see-Nile (senile) thing to do.

What soap is hardest? Cast-steel (Castile).

Why is the Bank of England like a thrush? Because it often changes its notes.

Why is Canada like courtship? Because it borders on the United States.

Who were the original bog-trotters? The Fen-ians.

Why is a ship in a stream like a nail? Because it is often driven into Deal.

Why is Paris like the letter F? Because it is the capital of France.

Why is the Brooklyn Bridge like merit? Because it is very often passed over.

Why do so many people in China travel on foot? Because there is but one coach in China (Cochin China).

CHAPTER VII

LITERARY CONUNDRUMS

WHAT American poet may be considered equal to three-fifths of the poets ancient and modern? Poe.

The names of which two Greek poems will you mention on alluding to their author's peculiar manner and indisposition? Homer's Odd-I-see and Ill-I-add.

Why is an unskillful physician like Peleus' son, Achilles? Because both have "sent many souls to Hades ere their time."

What injury did the Lavinia of Thomson's "Seasons" do to young Palemon? She pulled his ears and trod on his corns.

If a tough beefsteak could speak, what English poet would it mention? Chaw-sir (Chaucer).

Was it John Byrom who, in comparing two celebrated musicians, said one was Tweedledum, the other only Tweedledee? If so, state which of these two names was the more difficult to write. Tweedledum, because he wrote the other with more e's (ease).

Why was it a mistake to imagine that Robinson Crusoe's island was uninhabited? Because the very first thing he saw upon landing was a great swell a pitchin' into a little "cove" on the shore.

What prescription is the best for a poet? A composing draught.

Why is an author the most wonderful man in the world? Because his tale (tail) comes out of his head.

Why was Bulwer more likely to get tired of novel-writing than Warren? Because Bulwer wrote "Night and Morning," Warren only "Now and Then."

What author would eye-glasses and spectacles mention to the world if they could only speak? Eusebius (you see by us).

Why is a wax candle like Dickens' last work? Because it's a cereal (serial) work.

When is a slug like a poem of Tennyson's? When it's in a garden ("Enoch Arden").

How do we know Lord Byron was good-tempered? Because he always kept his choler (collar) down.

How can you instantly convict one of error when stating who was the earliest poet? By mentioning one Prior.

What was the most melancholy fact in the history of Milton? That he could "recite" his poems, but not re-sight himself.

Why do we speak of poetic fire? Because if the ancient Scandinavians had their "Skalds," we have also had our Burns.

What English poet does a mummy resemble? Dryden (dried-'un).

What lady of the Dante family is most often spoken of? Ann-dante.

Why are baldheaded men in danger of dying? Because "Death loves a shining mark."

What poem of Hood's resembles a tremendous Roman nose? "The Bridge of Sighs" (the bridge of size).

Why was Dickens a greater writer than Shakespeare? Shakespeare wrote well, but Dickens wrote Weller.

What proof have we that Cowper was in debt? He "oh'd for a lodge in some vast wilderness."

Why should the poet have expected the woodman to "spare that tree?" Because he thought he was a good feller (fellow).

Why are the relics of the departed like a man whose pocket has been robbed and the thief escaped? Because they have both felt "the touch of a vanished hand."

When is a pie like a poet? When it's Browning.

What best describes and most impedes a Pilgrim's Progress? Bunyan (bunion).

Why are Addison's works like a looking-glass? Because in them we see the "Spectator."

Was Othello thinking of his wife when he killed her? No, 's mother.

What toe would you rather kiss than the Pope's? Mrs. Beecher S-towe.

Who was the first whistler, and what tune did he whistle? The wind,—"Over the Hills and Far Away."

Who wrote most, Dickens or Bulwer?

Dickens. He wrote "All the Year Round," while Bulwer wrote "Night and Morning."

What countryman was Burns? A Scorchman.

What change of identity did the "Beggar's Opera" effect? It made Gay rich, and Rich gay.

When was the greatest destruction of poultry? When King Claudius of Denmark "did murder most foul."

Why are the abbreviations of degrees tacked on to a man's name? To show that he is a man of letters.

"Why," asked Moore, the poet, "is love like a potato?" Because it shoots from the eyes, "and," added Byron, "gets less by pairing."

If Falstaff had been musical what instrument would he have chosen after dinner? The sackbut.

Why is it almost certain that Shakespeare was a broker? Because no man has furnished so many stock quotations.

Why is a statistician like a writer of one

of the Six Best Sellers? Because he is the author of well-figured fiction.

Why are Parliamentary reports called "Blue Books?" Because they are never re(a)d.

Why is an architect like a newspaper writer? Because he gets so much "per column" for his work.

Why was Blackstone like an Irish vegetable? Because he was a common tatur (commentator).

Is there any bird which can recite the "Lays of Ancient Rome?" Yes, certainly, Macaw-lays.

Why cannot the Irish perform the play of "Hamlet?" Because they cannot help making "Aphalia" (a failure) of the heroine.

What was Othello's occupation in Venice? That of a lawyer, because he was attorney-general (a tawny general).

If you took off your boot and put your foot in the fire, what opera of Verdi's would it instantly make you? Rigoletto (wriggle-a-toe).

Why are unsuccessful contestants for a

prize like Shakespeare? Because they have made "Much Ado About Nothing."

What is the difference between living "in marble halls" and aboard ship? In the former you have "vassals and serfs at your side," and in the latter you have vessels and surfs at your side.

Why is it quite reasonable that Dickens' later plots should be complicated? Because one of his earlier works was all of a twist (Oliver Twist).

Why have the inhabitants of the city of Boston less need of foreign bards than those of any other city? Because they can always find poetry in their own "Holmes."

Why is a competent lawyer like a bloodstone set in jet? Because he is deep read (red) in Blackstone.

NAMES OF AUTHORS

A slang expression. Dickens.

A brighter and a smarter one. Whittier.

Put a grain 'twixt an ant and a bee, and a well-beloved poet you'll see. Bryant.

It comes from a pig.   Bacon.

II.   Mark Twain.

A ten-footer whose name begins with fifty.   Longfellow.

Part of a lady's wearing apparel used long ago.   Spencer.

What is an oyster heap likely to become? Shelley.

It is worn on the head.   Hood.

A worker in precious metals.   Goldsmith.

What is the value of a word?   Wordsworth.

A domestic animal.   Lamb.

He mends and repairs.   Cooper.

Many people would like to kiss him. Pope.

It pertains to a monastery.   Abbott.

A domestic servant.   Cook.

Which is the better playwright, William Shakespeare or Brinsley Sheridan?   Willis.

Part of a fish.   Finley.

What the children delight in at the seashore.   Sands.

CHAPTER VIII

CONUNDRUMS ON THE ALPHABET

What word is it of only three syllables which combines in it twenty-six letters? Alphabet.

Which word in the English language contains the greatest number of letters? Disproportionableness.

What is the best bet ever made? The alphabet.

When were there only two vowels? In the days of No-a, before U and I were born.

When will there be but twenty-five letters in the alphabet? When U and I are one.

Why is U the gayest letter in the alphabet? Because it is always in fun.

Why is T the happiest letter in the alphabet? Because it is next to you.

Which are the two hottest letters in the alphabet? K N (cayenne).

Why is O the most charitable letter in the alphabet? Because it is found oftener than any other letter d-o-ing g-oo-d.

Why is the letter T like matrimony? It is the end of quiet and the beginning of trouble.

Why is a farmer surprised at the letter G? It converts oats into goats.

When was B the first letter of the alphabet? In the days of No-a.

What step must I take to remove A from the alphabet? B-head it.

Why is A like a honeysuckle? Because a "B" follows it.

Why is the letter W like a scandal? Because it makes ill will.

Why are two t's like hops? Because they make beer better.

Spell enemy in three letters. No, not N M E; it's F O E.

Spell auburn locks in two letters. S and Y.

Spell brandy in three letters. B R and Y, and O D V.

What must you add to nine to make it six? S, for IX with S is six.

If you asked the alphabet to come to dinner, which letters could not accept your kind invitation till later in the evening? The last six, as they couldn't come till after T.

How can you tell a girl of the name of Ellen that she is everything that is delightful in eight letters? U-r-a-bu-t-l-n.

What is that which occurs twice in a moment and not once in a thousand years? The letter M.

Why is A like twelve o'clock? Because it's the middle of day.

Why is a false friend like the letter P? Because, though always first in pity, he is ever last in help.

Why is the letter P like a Roman emperor? Because it's near O (Nero).

Why is a fish-hook like the letter F? Because it will make an eel feel.

What letter is that which is invisible, but never out of sight? I.

How would you express in two letters that

you were twice the bulk of your companion? I W (I double you).

What two Christian names read the same both ways? Hannah and Anna.

Why is the Isthmus of Suez like the first U in cucumber? Because it's between two seas (c's).

What word is there of eight letters which has five of them the same? Oroonoko.

Why is O the noisiest of all vowels? Because you cannot make a horrid loud noise without it, whilst all the others are in*audible*.

What word contains the five vowels in their order? Facetious.

Why is I the luckiest of all the vowels? Because it is in the center of bl*i*ss, whilst E is in h*e*ll, and all the others are in p*u*rg*a*t*o*ry.

What must all the letters of the alphabet be in order to possess infinite sagacity? Wise (y's).

Y y u r y y u b i c u r y y for me. Too wise you are, two wise you be; I see you are too wise for me.

What are those things, which, though they

appear twice in every day, and twice in every week, yet are only seen twice in a year? Vowels.

What letter in the alphabet is necessary to make a shoe? The last.

What word of six letters admits of five successive elisions, leaving at each abbreviation a well-known word? Brandy—brand—bran—ran—an—a.

Name two English words, one of which, being of one syllable only, shall contain more letters than the other of five syllables? Strength—Ideality.

Why is a glass-blower the most likely person to set the alphabet off at a gallop? Because he can make a D-canter.

What word of six letters contains six words besides itself, without transposing a letter? Herein—he—her—here—ere—rein—in.

Is there a word in the English language which contains all the vowels? Yes, unquestionably.

Why is quizzing like the letter **D** on horseback? It is deriding (D riding).

When did " Chicago " begin with a " C "

and end with an "e"? Chicago always began with a "C" and end always began with an "e."

There is an English word of more than two letters, of which la is the middle, is the beginning, and is the end, though there is but one "a" and one "l" in the word. What is it? Island, of which "la" is the middle, "is" the beginning, "and" is the end.

What word is there of five letters, that, by taking two away, leaves but one? Stone.

What word of one syllable, if you take two letters from it, remains a word of two syllables? Plague; ague.

Why is the letter E a gloomy and discontented vowel? Because, though never out of health and pocket, it never appears in spirits.

Why are the fourteenth and fifteenth letters of the alphabet of more importance than the others? Because we cannot get ON well without them.

Why is the letter D like a squalling child? Because it makes ma mad.

What river is ever without a beginning and ending? S-ever-n.

Which is the coldest river? The Ice is (Isis).

What word of ten letters can be spelled with five? XPDNC (expediency).

What word of four syllables represents Sin riding on a little animal? Synonymous (Sin on a mouse).

Why is an island like the letter T? Because it is in the midst of water (wa-t-er).

Like what four letters of the alphabet is a honey-producing insect when in small health? Like A B C D (a bee seedy).

Why is the letter S like a sewing-machine? Because it makes needles needless.

Why is an uncomfortable seat like comfort? Because it is devoid of e's (ease).

What two letters do boys delight in to the annoyance of their elders? Two t's (to tease).

What single word would you put down for $40 borrowed from you? XL lent (excellent).

What letter is the pleasantest to a deaf woman? A, because it makes her hear.

What word is it, which, by changing a single letter, becomes its own opposite? United, untied.

Why should the male sex avoid the letter A? Because it makes men mean.

Why is a schoolmistress like the letter C? Because she forms lasses into classes.

Why is the letter W like a maid of honor? Because it is always in waiting.

Spell an interrogation with one letter. Y (why?).

Why is the letter T like an amphibious animal? Because it lives both in earth and water.

Why is the nose on your face like the v in civility? Because it's between two eyes (i's).

Take away one letter from me, and like Macbeth I murder; take away two, and I probably shall die, if my whole does not save me. Kill-ill-skill.

There is a word of three syllables, from

which if you take away five letters a male will remain; if you take away four, a female will be conspicuous; if you take away three, a great man will appear; and the whole word shows what Joan of Arc was? He, her, hero, heroine.

What letter in the Dutch alphabet will name an English lady of title? A Dutch-S.

Why is the letter D like a hoop of gold? Because we can't be wed without it.

Why is the letter K like a pig's tail? Because it is the end of pork.

How do you spell "blind pig" in two letters? P G, pig without an I.

Why is a horse like the letter O? Because Gee makes it Go.

Why is the figure 9 like a peacock? It is nothing without its tail.

When is the letter L like a piece of unparalleled generosity? When it enables a lady to make over a lover.

Why is the letter F like a cow's tail? It is the end of beef.

Describe a suit of old clothes in two letters? C D (seedy).

Make five less by adding to it. V, IV.

Why is the letter S like a pert repartee? Because it begins and ends in sauciness.

What small animal is turned into a larger one by beheading it? Fox—ox.

Why are sidewalks in winter like music? If you don't C sharp, you will B flat.

Why is a pensive widow like the letter X? Because she's never inconsolable.

What two letters express the most agreeable people in the world? U and I.

How does the letter Y work an impossibility? It makes a lad into a lady.

Tie a cross to a monkey and the animal will be transposed into a point. Add X to ape, and you obtain apex.

Why is the letter N like a pig? Because it makes a sty nasty.

Why is it that I cannot spell Cupid? When I get to C U (see you) I forget everything else.

Why is the letter B like a fire? Because it makes oil boil.

Why is the letter R a profitable letter? Because it makes ice into rice.

Why is the letter T like Easter? Because it's the last of Lent.

When does a blacksmith make a row in the alphabet? When he makes a poke-R and shove-L.

What did the old woman say when she looked into the empty flour barrel? O I C U R M T.

Why did Noah object to the letter D? Because it made the ark dark.

Why are stars like an old barn? Because there are r, a, t, s in both.

What are the worst letters of recommendation? I O U.

Why is the letter D like a sailor? It follows the C (sea).

If I were in the sun and you out of it, what would the sun become? Sin.

I am neither flesh, fish, nor fowl, yet I frequently stand upon one leg; if you behead me I stand upon two; if you again decapitate me I stand upon four. I shall think you are related to me if you do not now recognize me. Glass—lass—ass.

Three letters three rivers proclaim. Ex, Wye, Dee.

Three letters an ode give to fame. L E G (elegy).

Three letters an attribute name. N R G (energy).

Three letters a compliment claim. U X L (You excel).

The beginning of eternity,
The end of time and space,
The beginning of every end,
The end of every race. Letter E.

One letter's a tree? U (yew).
One means to agree? A (aye).
One is to drink? T (tea).
One a bird, think? J (jay).

Now of letters that rhyme
You must guess them in time;
One is an insect busy all day? B (bee).
One is a river that wends on its way? D (Dee).
One is a slang word it is best not to say. G (Gee).
These two letters are not at all hard? E Z (easy).

These letters form a literary composition. S A (essay).

These letters will decompose? D K (decay).

These letters form a material to wear? P K (pique).

These letters do the best of all? X L (excel).

These letters form a tree? L M (elm).

The meaning of these letters is not full? M T (empty).

CHAPTER IX

GENERAL CONUNDRUMS

WHY is a baby like a sheaf of wheat? Because it is first cradled, then threshed, and afterward becomes the flower of the family.

What is it that is queer about flowers? They shoot before they have pistils.

What is the worst thing to catch afire? Nothing.

Why is a man who has parted from his bed like one obliged to keep it? He is bed-ridden.

What is the oldest coupler in use? The wedding ring.

Why are hot rolls like caterpillars? Because they make the butterfly.

What is the difference between a mouse and a young lady? The one harms the cheese, the other charms the " he's."

When is a man thinner than a lath? When he is a-shaving.

Why is a pretty young lady like a wagon-wheel? Because she is surrounded by felloes (fellows).

Of what religious persuasion is the sea? A Quaker—for it has a broad brim.

Though I dance at a ball, yet am I nothing at all. A shadow.

What is that which, though black itself, enlightens the world? Ink.

When is a sailor not a sailor? When he's a-board.

What is the difference between a chess-player and an habitual toper? One watches the pawn, the other pawns the watch.

Which animal is the heaviest in all creation? A le(a)d horse.

What sort of tune do we all enjoy most? For-tune, made up of bank-notes.

Why is a spendthrift, with regard to his fortune, like the water in a filter? Because he soon runs through it, and leaves many matters behind to settle.

Why is English grammar like gout? Because it's torture (taught yer).

Why is an office with no work to do like a good dinner eaten by an invalid? Because it's a sign-o'-cure (sinecure).

Why is a shoeblack like an editor? Because he polishes the understandings of his patrons.

Why is opening a letter like taking a very queer method of entering a room? Because it is breaking through the sealing (ceiling).

Why are persons with short memories like office-holders? Because they are always for-getting everything.

What word is it which expresses two things we men all wish to get, one bringing the other, but which if we do get them, the one bringing the other, we are unhappy? Miss-fortune.

When is sugar like a pig's tooth? When in a hog's head.

Why is a joint company not like a watch? Because it does not go after it is wound up.

When may a man be said to be personally involved? When he is wrapped up in himself.

What wind should a hungry sailor wish for? One that blows fowl and chops about.

Why are bookkeepers like chickens? Because they have to scratch for a living.

Why do British soldiers never run away? Because they belong to the standing army.

What part of a car resembles a person? The wheel, because it is tired.

On which side of a pitcher is the handle? The outside.

When may a chair be said to dislike you? When it can't bear you.

What is that which divides by uniting and unites by dividing? The scissors.

Why are young children like castles in the air? Because their existence is only in-fancy.

Why is a proud girl like a music book? She is full of airs.

Why is a short negro like a white man? Because he is not at all black (not a tall black).

Why are bells the most obedient of inanimate things? Because they make a noise whenever they are told (tolled).

Why is the most discontented man the most easily satisfied? Nothing satisfies him.

Why are ripe potatoes in the ground like thieves? They ought to be taken up.

Why is it unjust to blame cabmen for cheating us? We call them to take us in.

Why are weary people like carriage wheels? Because they are tired.

Why does a tall man eat less than a short man? Because he makes a little go a long way.

What is the dryest subject? The mummy.

When are candles and women most alike? When sputtering.

Why are confectioners so much sought for? Because they serve kisses.

How many sides has a pitcher? Two, inside and outside.

What is wind like in a storm? Like to blow your hat off.

What is the difference between an honest and dishonest laundress? One irons your linen, the other steals it.

When is a policeman very like a rain-beau? When he appears after the storm is over.

Where are we most likely to find the sky blue? The nearer we go to the Milky Way.

What is the difference between a wealthy toper and a skillful miner? One turns his gold into quarts, the other turns his quartz into gold.

Why is an orange like a church steeple? Because we have a peel from it.

Why is the tolling of a bell like the prayer of a hypocrite? Because it's a solemn sound from a thoughtless tongue.

Why is a shoemaker like a true lover? Because he's faithful to the last.

What is the difference between a honeycomb and a honeymoon? One is made up of a lot of little cells, the other is one enormous sell only.

Why is the crabbed old bachelor who made the above conundrum like a harp struck by lightning? Because he is a blasted lyre.

When is truth not truth any longer? When it lies at the bottom of a well.

What should a clergyman preach about? About a quarter of an hour.

When is a man's pastor really and truly his brother? When he's his pa's son (parson).

What is the best way to hide a bear; it doesn't matter how big he is—the bigger the better? Skin him.

Why are sentries like day and night? Because when one comes the other goes.

When does the eagle turn carpenter? When he soars (saws) the woods—and plains.

Which one of a carpenter's tools is coffee like? An axe with a dull edge, because it must be ground before it can be used.

Why is it vulgar to send a telegram? Because it is making use of flash language.

Why is a spider a good correspondent? Because he drops a line by every post.

What is the difference between a correspondent and a corespondent? One is a man who does write (right), and the other a man who does wrong.

What kind of servants are best for hotels? The inn-experienced.

What sort of a day would be a good one to run for a cup? A muggy one.

Why are sugar-plums like racehorses? Because the more you lick them the faster they go.

Why ought a greedy man to wear a plaid waistcoat? To keep a check on his stomach.

When a church is burning, what is the only part that runs no chance of being saved? The organ, because the engine can't play upon it.

When are sheep stationery? When turned into pens, and into paper when folded.

What key in music will make a good officer? A Sharp Major.

What is the key-note to good manners? B Natural.

In what key should a declaration of love be made? Be mine, ah! (B Minor).

Why do teetotalers run such a slight risk of drowning? Because they are so accustomed to keep their noses above water.

What kind of a cravat would a hog be most likely to choose? A pigs-tye, of course.

Why is a flirt like an india-rubber ball? Because she's empty, yet full of bounce.

When is a butcher a thorough thief? When he steals a knife and cuts away with it.

Why is a field of grass like a person older than yourself? Because it's past-your-age (pasturage).

If Old Nick were to lose his tail, where should he go to supply the deficiency? To a grog shop, because there bad spirits are retailed.

What sense pleases you most in an unpleasant acquaintance? Absence.

Why is an abstract of a lecture like a sentimental boy and girl kissing? Because it's a syllabus (silly buss).

Why is a pictorial riddle like a second kiss? Because it's a rebus (re-buss).

Why is the latest thing in a fashionable gown like the South African bushman's club? Because it's "perfectly stunning."

Why is a department store like a country

sewing circle? Because it has so many notions.

Why is a music teacher like a baseball coach? Because he frequently says, "Try that last run over again."

What is the difference between a bright scholar and shoe polish? One shines at the head, the other at the foot.

What is a better investment the worse it is? A tenement.

When does a musician fail? When he is unable to discount his notes.

Why is a jeweler like a prisoner in solitary confinement? Because he has too much time on his hands.

When is a doctor like a cross-tempered man? When he is losing his patients.

Under what circumstances are a builder and a newspaper reporter equally likely to fail? When they make up stories without foundations.

Why is a hack-horse a miserable creature? Because his mind is always on the rack, and his only consolation is woe (whoa!).

Why is a good joke like the modern ballot

box? Because it is the greatest repeater known to history.

Why is a dressmaker braver than an actor? Because she is not afraid of the hook.

Why is the aspiring poet about to approach an editor with his verses like a consumptive? Because he's going into a decline.

Why is turkey a fashionable bird? Because he always appears well dressed.

Why should a candle-maker never be pitied? Because all his works are wicked, and all his wicked works, when brought to light, are only made light of.

How would you increase the speed of a very slow boat? Make her fast.

Why is matrimony like an invested city? Because when we are out of it we wish to be in it, and when we are in it we wish to be out of it.

Why is a person of short stature like an almanac? Because he is often looked over or over-looked.

Why is a certain kind of coach like the exclusive option on a certain girl's kisses? Because it's an omnibus.

Why are seasick excursionists like a strong opposition in Congress? Because they are opposed to the motion.

Why is the aëronaut whose airship plows into the earth like a successful speculator? Because he has taken a flier in real estate.

Why are airship inventors like musicians? Because they bend all their energies to the conquest of the air.

Why are the speeches of an orator heard through a phonograph like the State House dome? Because they are hollow but illuminating.

Why is a discredited politician like an unpopular dentist? Because each has lost his pull.

Why are seeds when sown like gate-posts? Because they propagate.

Why is fashion like a blank cartridge? Because it's all powder and puff.

Why is the Fourth of July like oysters? Because we can't enjoy it without crackers.

Why ought women to be employed in a post-office? Because they know how to manage the mails (males).

Why do the recriminations of married couples resemble the sound of waves on the shore? Because they are murmurs of the tied (tide).

What have you now before you which would give you a company, a veiled lady, and a noisy toy? Co-nun-drum.

Why is a mother rocking her child to sleep liable to arrest? Because she is engaged in a kid-napping project.

What is the cheapest candy? Horehound, because the advertisements of it read constantly, "Horehound drops 10 cents a lb."

Why does a rich lady act prudently by marrying a penniless man? Because she husbands her resources.

Why should a straw hat never be raised to a lady? Because, no matter how much you raise it, or how much she appreciates it, it is never felt.

When is a wall like a fish? When it is scaled.

Why is it impossible for a swell who lisps to believe in the existence of young ladies? Because he calls every Miss a Myth.

Why is a specimen of handwriting like a dead pig? Because it is done with the pen.

Why are good intentions like fainting ladies? Because all they want is carrying out.

What is it we all frequently say we will do and no one has ever yet done? Stop a minute.

Why can't a thief easily steal a watch? Because he must take it off its guard.

Why is a treadmill run by convicts like a true convert? Because its turning is the result of conviction.

Why is the rumseller's trade a profitable one to follow? Because, by conducting it with good spirits, he has more bar-gains than most others, and all his drafts (draughts) are paid.

Why is the inside of everything mysterious? Because we can't make it out.

What is that which a woman frequently

gives her lovely countenance to, yet never takes kindly? The small-pox.

Why is a bad gimlet like a prophesier of ill events? Because it is an auger-ill.

What is the strongest day? Sunday, because all of the others are "week" days.

What is the best way to make the hours go fast? Use the spur of the moment.

Why is the proprietor of a balloon like a phantom? Because he's an airy-naught (aëronaut).

Why is a fool in a high station like a man in a balloon? Because everybody appears little to him, and he appears little to everybody.

Why is an old coat like iron? Because it is a specimen of hard-ware.

Why is a leaky barrel like a coward? Because it runs.

If a man attempts to jump a ditch and falls, why is he likely to miss the beauties of summer? Because the fall follows right after the spring, unless he makes a summer-set between them.

What does an iron-clad vessel of war, with

four inches of steel plating and all its guns on board, weigh just before starting on a cruise? She weighs anchor.

Why is a washerwoman like Saturday? Because she brings in the close (clothes) of the week.

When is it a good thing to lose your temper? When it is a bad one.

Why should a man never marry a woman named Ellen? Because he rings his own (k)nell.

What is it which covers a multitude of sin(ner)s? The gravestone.

Why is a vessel being blown out to sea like a bankrupt householder? Because both submit to a forced sail.

Why is a rooster on a fency like a penny? Because his head's on one side and tail's on the other.

What is the military definition of a kiss? A report at headquarters.

Why are washerwomen foolish people? Because they put out their tubs to catch soft water when it rains hard.

What is smaller than a mite's mouth? What goes into it.

Why is love always represented as a child? Because he never reaches the age of discretion.

Why is a man hanged better than a vagabond? Because he has a visible means of support.

What is the difference between photography and whooping-cough? The one makes facsimiles, the other sick families.

Why is a dog like a man four feet ten inches tall? Because he stands over four feet.

Why does the mayor order the saloons closed after a great fire? That the people may not try to drown their losses.

What is it which more people lie under than upon? The gravestone.

What is it that opens to all comers, advertises only the doctors, and yet is good for everything that ails you? The grave.

Why is a bride, weary of her apartment home, like a wrecked automobile? They've both got flat tire.

Why is a gardener like a detective-story writer? Because he works up his plot.

Why is a widower in love again like a good gardener? Because he immediately removes his weeds.

Why can the weight of an illuminating argument never be accurately determined? Because as the hearer weighs the words the scales fall from his eyes.

How does the surgeon, whose bill for an operation has been delayed by executors, resemble his deceased patient? He feels terribly cut up.

How does the cavalryman whose horse has thrown him differ from the faithful orderly? He obeys orders from hind quarters, while the orderly obeys orders from headquarters.

What is the best place to sow wild oats? Near a bank.

Why is a conductor on a car like a firefly? Because he can make you a-light.

Why is an automobilist who exceeds the speed limit like a social reprobate? Because he's too fast.

Why is the divorce court like certain newspapers? Because it has a matrimonial co-respondents' (correspondence) section.

What is the longest word in the English language? Smiles, because it has a mile between its first and last letters.

Which is heavier, a pound of gold or a pound of feathers? A pound of feathers, which weigh a pound avoirdupois; a pound of gold is a pound troy.

What is the first thing you do when you get into bed? You make an impression.

Why is twice ten like twice eleven? Because twice ten is twenty, and twice eleven is twenty-two (too).

Why is a pretty girl's pleased-merry-bright-laughing-eye no better than an eye destroyed? Because it's an-eye-elated.

That which every one requires, that which every one gives, that which every one asks, and that which very few take? Advice.

When is a thief like a reporter? When he takes notes.

When is a nation like a baby? When it is in arms.

What does the lamp post become when the lamp is removed? A lamp lighter.

Why is a mother who spoils her child like a person building castles in the air? She indulges in-fancy too much.

When you listen to your little brother's drum, why are you like a just judge? Because you hear both sides.

What is the action of the moon? It affects physically the tide, and sentimentally the untied.

Why is a father who frequently thrashes his boy likely to be prosecuted? Because he exerts undue influence in the making of a will.

How should Messrs. Taft and Roosevelt now travel? By ex-Pres.

Why is a Wall Street lamb like a surgical convalescent? Because he's been operated on.

Why is the humiliated braggart like the small boy who has drunk the washing fluid? Because he has swallowed the lye.

Why is the fresh young upstart like an aërial postman? Because he's up and coming.

Why is an elevator man like an aëronaut? Because his life is all ups and downs.

What is the coldest place in an opera house? Z row.

What will eventually change the size of the auto? The demand for more gauge (mortgage) which the present fad creates.

Why is the nurse of an insane ward like a popular opera star? Because everybody's crazy about him.

Why do love letters have a financial value? Because they are promissory notes.

When are words musical? When they have a ring to them.

When is a woman a live wire? When she's shocking.

Why is it easy to practice rotation of crops on the prairies? Because of the frequency of whirlwinds there.

Why is an astronomer like a theatrical manager? Because he's always looking for new stars.

Why is an airship bequeathed you by your father like the portrait of an ancestor? Because it is a family heirloom.

When is a lady's arm not a lady's arm? When it is a little bare.

When is a fish above its station? When it rises and takes a fly.

When is a boy not a boy? When he is a regular brick.

When is a piece of wood like a queen? When it is made into a ruler.

When is a skein of thread like the root of an oak? When it is full of knots.

What is that which has a mouth but never speaks, and a bed but never sleeps in it? A river.

Why should you never have a tailor who does not understand his trade? Because you would get bad habits from him.

What is the difference between a sailor and a soldier? One tars his ropes, the other pitches his tent.

Which is the ugliest hood ever worn? Falsehood.

What is the best thing to make in a hurry? Haste.

Why are cobblers like a famous physician?

They are skilled in the art of healing (heeling).

What pen ought never to be used for writing? A sheep pen.

When is a subject beneath one's notice? When it is under consideration.

Why is a loyal gentleman like a miser? He knows the value of his sovereign.

When is a bill not a bill? When it is dew.

What is the proper newspaper for invalids? The Weekly News.

When is a pint of milk not a pint? When it's condensed.

What tune makes everybody glad? Fortune.

What is it that has four legs and only one foot? A bedstead.

Why is attar of roses never moved without orders? Because it is sent wherever it goes.

What goes most against a farmer's grain? His reaper.

What precious stone is like the entrance to a field? A-gate.

When is a man like frozen rain? When he is hale (hail).

Which of the stars should be subject to the game laws? Shooting stars.

What garden crop would save draining? Leeks.

When does a cook break the game laws? When she poaches eggs.

When is a river like a young lady? When it is crossed.

Why is a carpenter like a languid dandy? Because he often feels a great deal bored.

When does a donkey weigh least? When he is within the pound.

What is the last blow a defeated ship gives in battle? Striking her own flag.

What had better be done when there is a great rent on a farm? It had better be sewn (sown).

Why should onions be planted near the potatoes in a garden? So that the onions may have a tear-producing effect upon the eyes of the potatoes and make them self-irrigating.

Why may not the proprietor of a forest fell his own timber? Because no one is allowed to cut when it is his own deal.

What is the oldest piece of furniture in the world? The multiplication table.

Which is the greatest number, six dozen dozen or half a dozen dozen? Six dozen dozen, of course.

What is that which, the more you take from it, the larger it grows? A hole.

If a bee could stand on its hind legs, what blessing would it invoke? A bee-attitude.

Why is a blockhead deserving of promotion? Because he is equal to any post.

Why is an artist stronger than a horse? Because he can draw Windsor Castle all by himself, and take it clean away in his pocket if necessary.

Why is money often moist? Because it is frequently dew in the morning, and mist at night.

Why are lawyers such uneasy sleepers? Because they lie first on one side, and then on the other, and remain wide awake all the time.

And what do they do when they die? Lie still.

When is a lawyer like a donkey? When drawing a conveyance.

What proverb must a lawyer *not* act up to? He must not take the will for the deed.

Why will scooping out a turnip be a noisy process? Because it makes it hollow.

When was beef the highest? When the cow jumped over the moon.

What is the difference between one yard and two yards? A fence.

Why is a straw hat like kissing through the telephone? Because neither is felt.

Why is your shadow like a false friend? Because it only follows you in sunshine.

Why is your nose in the middle of your face? Because it is the scenter.

If a woman asks her blind lover the color of a flower, what would he say? "I have no i-dea."

When are lawyers circumstances? When they alter cases.

Why is a dog's tail like an expressman? It keeps a-waggin'.

Why are chickens liberal? They give a *peck* when they take a *grain*.

What animals are in the clouds? Raindear.

Why is a young lawyer in his office like one of his chickens roosting on his neighbor's fence? He has no business there.

What is the difference between perseverance and obstinacy? One arises from a strong *will*, the other from a strong *won't*.

In what color should friendship be kept? In violet.

What is the noblest musical instrument? An upright piano. What the vilest? A lyre.

How do seamstresses resemble rascals? They cut and run.

Why is a Bostonian's brain like a book of conundrums? Because it is full of notions.

Why is a fortunate man like a straw in the water? Because he goes on swimmingly.

Why is the man who falls in the kennel approved of? Because he's add-mir'd.

Why is an organ an enemy to religion? Because it stands against the communion.

Why are sharpers like sparrows? Because they feather their nests.

Why is a looking-glass very complaisant? Because it always does as the company does.

Why is a newspaper like a lame man? Because it generally lies.

Why is a staircase like a back-biter? Because its rail's against you.

Why is a high wind like a dumb man in distress? Because it makes moving signs.

Why are sheep the most dissipated of animals? They *gambol* all their youth, live by the turf, the best of them are blacklegs, and they get fleeced at last.

Why is a bald-headed man like a hunting dog? He makes a little *hare* go a great way.

Why is a horse that is constantly rid, though never fed, never starved? Because he's never without a bit.

Why is a sleepy servant like a warming pan? Because he's in bed before his master.

Why is a rich farmer like a man with bad teeth? Because he has a good many achers.

Why is an apple like a good song? Because it is encored.

Why is an eyelid like the wadding to a gun? Because it covers the ball.

Why is a smith like a ferryman? Because his business is to work ore.

Why is a garter like the gates of a slaughter house? Because it holds the stock in (stocking).

Why is a holly bush like a corpse? Because it is or will be berry'd.

Why is an apron like peas? Because it is gathered.

Why, when a very fat man gets squeezed coming out of the opera, does it make him complimentary to the ladies? Because the pressure makes him flatter.

Why are a couple of first-rate breech-loaders like two beautiful young ladies? Because they're pair-o'-guns (paragons).

Why is a woman's beauty like a gold coin? Because when once changed it soon goes.

What herb is most injurious to a lady's beauty? Thyme.

When is a superb woman like bread? When given as a toast.

Why is a lover's heart like a whale? Because it's a secreter (sea creatur') of great sighs (size).

How many wives are you allowed by the Prayer-book? Sixteen, viz.: Fo(u)r better, fo(u)r worser, fo(u)r richer, fo(u)r poorer; total, sixteen.

Why is paper like a beggar? Because it is composed of rags.

Why can Satan never be uncivil? Because the Imp o' Darkness can never be Imp o' Light.

Who is the man who carries everything before him? The footman.

Why is a pen manufacturer a corrupt man? Because he makes people steal (steel) pens and tells them they do write (right).

What is the greatest eye-sore in a farmyard? A pig-sty.

What is better than God, worse than the devil, what the dead live on, and the living would die if they lived on? Nothing.

Why is a prudent man like a pin? Because his head prevents him from going too far.

Whence proceeds the eloquence of a lawyer? From his mouth.

At what time by the clock is a pun the most effective? When it strikes one.

Why is a dead hen better than a live one? Because she will lay wherever you put her.

Why is a true and faithful friend like a garden seed? Because you never know the value of either until they are put under ground.

What benefit can be derived from a paper of pins? They will give you many good points.

What kind of a cat do we generally find in a large library? A catalogue.

Why is it difficult to flirt on mail steamers? Because all the mails (males) are tied up in bags.

What kind of a swell luncheon would hardly be considered a grand affair? A luncheon of dried apples and warm water, which is really a swell affair.

Why is a boy like a puppy? Because he's a younker (young cur).

What is that thing which we all eat and

drink, although it is often a man and often a woman? A toast.

How do eggs show their anger on being called Heggs? By becoming eggs-aspirated (exasperated).

On what side of a church does a yew-tree grow? The outside.

Why is a man whose "heart is in his mouth" through fright, like a cabbage? Because his heart's in his head.

Why is a shoemaker more charitable than another man? Because he is ready to give any man a lift.

Why is a picture like a fine woman? Because it's framed to please.

Why is a cunning man like a shoemaker? Because he'll pump you.

Why is a fiddle-maker like an apothecary? Because he'll send you a vial in.

Why would a pelican make a good lawyer? He knows how to stretch his bill.

When is a man incapable of performing a bare-faced action? When he wears a heavy beard and a mustache.

Why is a thief like a philosopher? Because he is given to fits of abstraction.

Why is it illegal for a man to possess a short walking stick? Because it can never be-long to him.

Why is a person who asks questions the strangest of all individuals? Because he is the querist.

What is that which travels about, goes much up and down, and wears shoes, but never had any shoes? A football.

Why are the pages of a book like the days of a man? Because they are numbered.

What word makes you sick if you leave out one of its letters? Music.

Why is a race at a circus like a big conflagration? Because the heat is in tents (intense).

Which is the left side of a plum pudding? The part that is not eaten.

Why is a man who runs in debt like a clock? He runs on tick.

Why is a bee-hive like a spectator? Because it is a bee-holder (beholder).

Why are fixed stars like pen, ink, and paper? Because they are stationary (stationery).

Why is a cook like a barber? He dresses hare (hair).

Why is a waiter like a race-horse? He often runs for a plate or a cup.

Why is a good story like a church bell? Because it is often tolled (told).

What is the weight of the moon? Four quarters.

How can you distinguish a fashionable man from a tired dog? One wears an entire costume; the other simply pants.

What is the difference between a new sponge and a fashionable man? If you well wet one it makes it swell, but if you well wet the other it takes all the swell out of him.

If I were to see you riding on a donkey, what fruit should I be reminded of? A pair (pear).

Why are cats like unskillful surgeons? Because they mew-till-late and destroy patience (mutilate and destroy patients).

When may you be said literally to "drink

in" music? When you have a piano for-tea (forte).

What is the difference between a professional pianoforte player, and the one who hears him? One plays for his pay, the other pays for his play.

Why is a thief like a bolus given to a lady? Because he's a pilferer (pill for her).

Why is a dead doctor like a dead duck? Because they have both done quacking.

Why is a commercial traveler whose "walk in life" is selling eggs, certain to be successful? Because he shows a good egg-sample from egg-sell-ent motives (example from excellent motives).

Why is an egg overdone like an egg underdone? Because it's hardly done.

What is most like a hen stealing? Why, a cock-robin.

Why have chickens no fear of a future state? Because they have their next world in this (necks twirled).

By what female name would an egg object to be called? Addle-laid (Adelaide).

Why ought cocks to be the smoothest birds

known? Because they always have a comb about them.

Why is a dirty man like flannel? Because he shrinks from washing.

What is the difference between the earth and the sea? One is dirty, the other tidy.

Why is geology considered a deep science? Because it penetrates deep into the earth.

Why was our last question like a young lady sitting on theological works? Because it was virgin on something serious.

When you see a lady in distress, what should you pull up, and what bury? You should pluck up courage and inter-fear (interfere) in her behalf.

What is the difference between a good and a bad governess? One teaches Miss, the other misteaches.

When may a man be said to be literally immersed in his business? When giving a swimming lesson.

What prevents a running river running right away? It is tied up.

What sort of a cold is necessary to insure your getting on well at Court? Influence-sir.

Why is a man taking a hedge at a single bound like one snoring? Because he does it in his-leap (his sleep).

Why are ladies like hinges? Because they are things to a door (adore).

What is that which never asks questions, yet requires many answers? The door-knocker.

Why is a door always in the subjunctive mood? Because it is always wood (would) —or should be.

Why is a new-born baby like a storm? Because it begins with a squall.

When is a schoolmaster like a man with one eye? When he has a vacancy for a pupil.

How do angry women prove themselves strong nerved? They exhibit their " presents of mind " by giving you a bit of it.

What soup would cannibals prefer? The broth of a boy.

What is the only form in this world which all nations, barbarous and civilized and otherwise, are agreed upon following? The female form.

Why is a comet more like a dog than the

dog-star? Because it has a tail and the dog-star hasn't.

Why is a watch-dog bigger by night than in the morning? Because he is let out at night and taken in in the morning.

Why is a dog biting his own tail like a good manager? Because he makes both ends meet.

When is a black dog not a black dog? When he is a grey-hound.

Why should you always choose white cows? Because it is no use milking those that are dun before you begin.

Why are two watches given as prizes like a happy married couple? Because though they are two, yet are they one (won).

Why is a human being like an earthen jug? Because both are made of clay.

Why is a man with corns on his feet like a certain favorite vegetable? Because he is a toe-martyr (tomato).

Why is a bald head like heaven? Because there is no parting or dyeing there.

Why is the meeting of lovers like a battle? Because there is an arm-y presentation.

Why is a young man who seldom attends church, sitting in the pulpit of a leaky church in a rain storm, like one who constantly attends church? Because he is sitting under the droppings of the sanctuary.

If a general should ask in vain for martial music, what word would embody his request? Conundrum (can none drum?).

Why is a fancy dancer like an old-fashioned country woman? Because she reels and spins.

In what constellation are the two shooting dogs which never go down? In Ursa Major, the pointers; they never go down because they are not setters.

What bird made the Yankee dish, bird's-nest pudding, and for what other bird was it made? Why, it was the cook who (cuckoo) made it, and for the swallow, of course.

Why are some ministers worse than Brigham Young? Because they have married more women than they can support, and would like to marry more.

In what respect does an attorney resemble a clergyman? He studies the law and profits (prophets).

What is the best way to raise strawberries? With a spoon.

Why is a man upstairs beating his wife an honorable man? Because he is *above* doing a mean action.

"Why," asks a disconsolate widow, "is venison like my late and never-sufficiently-to-be-lamented husband?" Because it is the dear (deer) departed.

What consolation has the homely girl? She will be a *pretty* old one if she lives long enough.

What moral sentence does a weathercock suggest? "It is a vain (vane) thing to a-spire."

What is that which if you take away all the letters remains the same? The postman.

Why is a correct knowledge of grammar indispensable to young clergymen? Because it leads to a(c)curacy.

Why is an extremely religious Roman Catholic lady only a very virtuous goose? Because she is so faithful to her proper gander (propaganda).

Why is a baker a most improvident person? Because he is continually selling that which he kneads himself.

Why is a good husband like dough? Because a woman needs him.

Why is it that the sun always rises in the East? Because the (y)east makes everything rise.

What is a very frequent mistake clergymen make in their sermons? Their being too long.

What is that if you take the whole away some remains? Whole-some.

Why is coal the most contradictory article known to commerce? Because when purchased it goes to the cellar (seller).

What is the difference between a baby and a shipwrecked sailor? One clings to its ma, and the other to his (s)par.

Why is a lance like the moon? Both are the glory of the knight.

When can you carry water in a sieve? When it is ice.

Why is a lame dog like the side of a mountain? It is a slow pup.

What is larger than a nutmeg? A nutmeg-grater.

When is it easiest to read? In the autumn when Nature turns the leaves.

Why do women seek husbands named William? That they may have a *Will* of their own.

Why is a steamboat a good place to sleep in? It leaves a-wake behind.

Who are the best astronomers? The stars, for they have studded the heavens for centuries.

What is it that goes up and down hill, but never moves? The road.

What is the difference between the Prince of Wales and a fountain? One is heir to the throne, the other thrown to the air.

Why is a negro woman like a doorway? Because she's a negress.

How does a sailor know there's a man in the moon? Because he has been to sea. Why didn't he stay there? Because he found it was full.

Why are you most likely to miss the 12:50 train? It is ten to one if you catch it.

Why should alchemists and astrologers be females? They are often Ann Elizas and Charlotte Anns from birth.

How does Patrick propose to get over his single blessedness? By proposing to Bridge-it.

Why is a kiss like a sermon? Because it requires two heads and an application.

Why should a man named Benjamin marry a girl named Annie? Because he would then be Bennie-fitted, and she Annie-mated.

State why a donkey browsing in a bed of thistles appears ill. Because he's a little down in the mouth, and looks rather seedy about the face.

Why am I, when prudently laying by money, like myself when foolishly squandering it? Because in either case I am—ass.

When is a teapot like a kitten? When you're teasin' it (your tea's in it).

Why does a puss purr? For an obvious pur-puss (purpose).

When is a fruit-stalk like a strong swimmer? When it stems the currants.

Why is lip-salve like a chaperon? Because it's meant to keep the chaps off.

Why are the bars of a convent like a blacksmith's apron? Because they keep the sparks off.

In what condition is a beer-barrel when it resembles old-fashioned curtains? When it's tap is dry (tapestry).

Why can the pall-bearers at a young lady's funeral never be dry? Because they have a gall on a bier between them.

What is the best day for making pancakes? Fry-day.

Why is a pair of skates like an apple? Because they have both occasioned the fall of man.

On a frosty day, what are the best fishes to fasten together? Skates, soles, an' (h)eels.

In what sort of syllables ought a parrot to be taught to speak? In polly-silly-bills.

Why is it dangerous for a teetotaler to have more than two reasons for the faith that is in him? Because three scruples make a dram.

What is the best key to a good dinner? Turkey.

Why is your favorite puppy like a doll? It is a pup-pet.

Which of the planets would a tortoise like best to live in? Herschel.

Why is a bullet like a tender glance? Because it pierces hearts.

What is the most suitable dance to wind up a frolic? A reel.

Why is a cook more noisy than a gong? One makes a din, the other a dinner.

What death does the sculptor die? He makes faces, and busts.

When may a room that is full of people be said to be empty? When there is not a *single* person in it.

Of what trade is the sun? A tanner.

When may a ship be said to be in love? When she is tender on a man-of-war.

When is she actively in love? When she seeks a mate.

When is she ambitiously in love? When she is making up to a peer.

When is she foolishly in love? When she is attached to a great buoy.

When is she absurdly in love? When she is h'anchoring after a heavy swell.

When is she demonstratively in love? When she hugs the shore.

When is she weakly in love? When she rests on the bosom of a little cove.

When is she treated too familiarly? When a smack follows her bow.

Why is a lame beggar inconsistent? He asks for alms when he wants legs.

Why has the acrobat such a wonderful digestion? Because he lives on ropes and poles, and thrives.

If the acrobat fell off his trapeze, what would he fall against? Against his inclination.

Why is a little dog's tail like the heart of a tree? Because it's farthest from the bark.

Why is there no such thing as an entire day? Because every day begins by breaking.

What is that which every living being has

seen, but will never see again? Yesterday.

What is that which *will be* yesterday, and *was* to-morrow? To-day.

What is better than presence of mind in a railway accident? Absence of body.

Why is traveling by the Subway dangerous? Because then you are sure to be run over by carriages and automobiles.

Why is it not flattery to tell an old lady that she is " as beautiful as an angel? " Because, if we believe what we read, the angels must be very ancient.

What is the superlative of temper? Tempest.

On what day of the year do women talk least? On the shortest day.

What sort of a musical instrument resembles a bad hotel? A vile-inn.

What is it which every one wishes for, and yet wants to get rid of as soon as it is obtained? A good appetite.

If a spider were late to dinner, what would he do? Take a fly.

Name the most unsociable things in the

world? Milestones; for you never see two of them together.

Why is swearing like an old coat? Because it is a bad habit.

Suppose you were to bore a hole exactly through the earth, starting from New York, and you went in at this end, where would you come out? Out of the hole.

What is the difference between a Roman Catholic priest and a Baptist? One uses wax candles and the other dips.

Why, when you paint a man's portrait, may you be described as stepping into his shoes? Because you make his feet-yours (features).

What is the very best and cheapest light, especially for painters? Daylight.

Why is a marine painter like a large vessel? Because he draws so much water.

Why is it extraordinary not to find a painter's studio as hot as an oven? Because it is there that he makes his bread.

Where should you feel for the poor? In your pocket.

What is the best way of making a coat

last? Make the trousers and waistcoat first.

What animals are admitted at the opera? White kids.

With what two animals do you always go to bed? Two calves.

Why are the actions of men like great rivers? Because we see the course that they take, but not the source whence they spring.

When is a young lady not a young lady? When she's a sweet tart (sweetheart).

Which is better, getting the girl of your choice or a shoulder of mutton? A shoulder of mutton; as nothing earthly can be better than getting her you love, and a shoulder of mutton is much better than nothing.

At what period in his sorrow does a widower recover from the loss of his dear departed? When he re-wives (revives).

Why are policemen particularly required in a hop ground? Because there are always so many people picking pockets there.

When is water most likely to escape? When it is only half-tide.

Plant a puppy, and what would come up? Dog would.

Why are artists like washerwomen? Because they are not satisfied until their works are "hung on the line."

Why is a man who never lays a wager as bad as a regular gambler? Because he is no better (bettor).

Why does the conductor cut a hole in your railroad ticket? To let you pass through.

Why should a man troubled with gout make his will? Because he will then have his leg at ease (legatees).

What is that which no one wishes to have, yet no one wishes to lose? A bald head.

Why are fixed stars like wicked old men? Because they sin-till-late (scintillate).

Why are very old people necessarily prolix and tedious? Because they die late (dilate).

A lady asked a gentleman how old he was. He answered, "My age is what you do in everything—excel (XL)."

Why is a mirror like a dissatisfied and ungrateful friend? Because, though you may positively load its back with silver, it will reflect on you.

Why is a butler like a mountain? Because he looks down on the valley (valet).

What is that which the fox has and the hare most wants? A brush.

What is the best way to keep a man's love? Not to return it.

Why is a wedding ring like eternity? Because it has no beginning and no end.

Why does a young lady prefer her mother's fortune to her father's? Because, though she likes patrimony, she still better likes matrimony.

Why is a deceptive woman like a seamstress? Because she is not what she seams (seems).

When does a man stand a good chance of being completely sewn up? When he has a stitch in his side.

Why does a dressmaker never lose her hooks? Because she has an eye to each of them.

What is the difference between a farmer and a seamstress? The farmer gathers what he sows, while the seamstress sews what she gathers.

If we were going to kill a conversational goose, what vegetable would she allude to? Ah!-spare-a-goose! (asparagus).

What is the best thing to do to enjoy the happiness of courting? To get a little gal-an'-try (gallantry).

How is it that the affections of young ladies, notwithstanding that they may protest and vow constancy, are always doubtful? Because they are only miss givings (misgivings).

Why may a beggar wear a very short coat? Because it will be long enough before he gets another.

What part of a lion is a new-born infant like? His tail, because it was never seen before.

Why can you never expect a fishmonger to be generous? Because his business makes him sell-fish.

Why is a judge's nose like the middle of the earth? Because it's the center of gravity.

What is the gentlest kind of spur? A whisper.

Why should not soldiers meddle with nut-crackers? Because they make the shells burst on the kernel (colonel).

Why is a hammer like a general? It goes to the head, and settles the point of a tack (attack).

What is the best material for kites? Fly-paper.

What two reasons are there why a young lady going to the altar is certainly going wrong? She is miss-taken and miss-led.

When does the tongue assume the functions of the teeth? When it back-bites.

What is a button? A small event that is always coming off.

What medicine ought to be given to misers? Anti-mony.

What was the cause of the potato rot? The rot-atory motion of the earth.

What is the end to which all like to come? A divid-end.

What is Hobson's choice? Mrs. Hobson.

Why should one never complain of the price of a car ticket? It is a *fare* thing.

Where does one see breakers ahead on land? In a railway station.

What is a heavy incidental expense? Having one's tooth filled.

What is the difference between forms and ceremonies? You sit upon one, and stand upon the other.

How do locomotives hear? Through their engin-eers.

What is the great motive for traveling? The loco-motive.

Why has a barber more than one life? Because he dyes (dies) very often.

How do you call the ship that carries more passengers than the *Olympic?* Court-ship.

Why is a high rate of fare on a railroad like an overloaded gun? Because it is too much for a charge.

When is a United States soldier like a man with a ragged coat? When he is out under arms.

When is a beaver hat a wide-awake? When it has lost its nap.

Why can hotel boarders dine off the gong? Because "it is a-rousing dinner."

Why is a retired actor like an extortioner? Because he is an ex-actor.

Who has most need to pray to be delivered from temptation? An editor, for he is beset by the "devil."

How can an actress appear in two pieces on the same evening? Because she's taking a part (taken apart).

Why is a watch like the moon? Because it presents halves and quarters and reports time.

Why is any divorced man like a man playing at ten pins? Because he has to pay an alimony (an alley-money).

Why is a woman, when blindfolded, like an ignorant school teacher? Because her pupils are kept in the dark.

Why is a ball discharged in the air like an article for soldiers' comfort? Because it is a blank hit (blanket).

Why is an honest poor man like a dishonest bankrupt man? Because they both fail to become rich.

Why is a beautiful woman at her marriage festival like one on horseback? Because she holds a bridal reign (bridle rein).

Why are the men appointed to wind up the affairs of a bank whose treasurer has defaulted, as bad as the treasurer himself? Because the receiver is as bad as the thief.

Why do architects make excellent actors? Because they are good at drawing houses.

Why is a blush an anomaly? Because a woman who blushes is admired for her cheek.

Why is a steel-trap like the small-pox? Because it is catching.

Why do girls kiss each other, and men not? Because girls have nothing better to kiss, and men have.

If I kiss a lady by mistake, what weapon do I use? A blunderbuss.

Why would young ladies of the present day make good pugilists? Because they are eager to enter the ring at sixteen, and are willing to make a match with a man twice their own size any day.

When is a man a muff? When he holds a lady's hand without squeezing it.

When is a man a spoon? When he touches a lady's two lips without kissing them.

How would you measure a lover's sincerity? By his sighs (size).

When is music like vegetables? When there is two beats (beets) to a measure.

Why is the *Outlook* like a man of fourscore? Because it's weekly.

Why is a false oath like a trial in the criminal court? Because it is per-jury.

Why are doctors always wicked men? Because the worse people are the more they are with them.

What sort of music should a girl sing whose voice is cracked and broken? Pieces.

What is better than an indifferent singer in a drawing room after dinner? A different one.

What animals always have gaiters on? Alligators.

What nation has always overcome in the end? Determination.

Why should you never sleep in a railway train? The train runs over sleepers.

What most frequently becomes a woman? A little girl.

What is an Englishman's notion of woman's mission? Sub-mission.

What remedy does an Irishman take for a scolding wife? He takes an e-lix-ir (he licks her).

What is the difference between a cloud of rain and a beaten child? One pours with rain, the other roars with pain.

What did the sunbeam say to the violet? "Wilt thou?" And she wilted.

What rose is "born to blush unseen"? Neg-roes.

What relation is a loaf of bread to a locomotive? The mother—bread being a necessity, a locomotive being an invention, and "Necessity is the mother of invention."

What is more moist than a young lady with a waterfall on her head, a cataract in her eye, a little lake on each cheek, high-tied shoes, and a crick in her back? A young lady with a notion (an ocean) in her head.

What is the best kind of agricultural fair? A farmer's very pretty daughter.

Why is a photograph like a member of Congress? Because it's a representative.

Why is a pelted actor like a pardoned criminal? Because he's glad to get off.

When is a bank note like iron? When it is forged.

Why is the sun like a good loaf? It is light when it rises.

Why may a dyspeptic hope for a long life? He can't die just (digest) now.

Why does a person who is ailing lose his sense of touch? Because he does not feel well.

If you were to swallow a man, what sort of man would you prefer? A little London porter.

Why should you never make love in the

country? Because corn has ears, potatoes eyes, and the beans talk.

Why is an aged man like a deserted house? His gait (gate) is broken, and his locks are few.

What did a blind man take at breakfast which restored his sight? A cup and saucer (saw, sir!).

Which is the laziest plant, and which the most active? The creeper and the running vine.

Why is an autoist whose machine has been completely wrecked like a reformed autoist? Because he has suddenly given up motoring.

What does a hen do when she stands on one foot? Lifts up the other.

Why should the largest tree be near a church? There should be no bigger tree (bigotry) there.

Why is a stupid servant like a church bell? He has to be often told (tolled).

Why are sailors in a leaky vessel like dancing masters? They depend on their pumps.

Why does a duck go into water? For diver's (diverse) reasons.

Why does a duck come out of water? For sun-dry (sundry) reasons.

What is the difference between a duck with one wing and one with two? Merely a difference of a pinion (opinion).

Why wasn't Peary buried in New York? He isn't dead yet.

When is the wind like a woodchopper? When it cuts.

What makes the ocean get angry? It has been crossed so often.

What is the characteristic of a watch? Modesty, as it keeps its hands before its face, and runs down its own works.

When is a clock on the stairs dangerous? When it runs down.

Why is a girl like an arrow? Because she is sure to be in a quiver till her bow comes, and can't go off without one.

Why are teeth like verbs? Because they are regular, irregular, and defective.

What hands are those which work night

and day, yet never wear out; which, although they strike, do not stop? Clock hands.

What's the difference between a gardener and a billiard marker? One minds his peas, the other his cues.

What is that which denotes the state of mind and of the body? The tongue.

Why are books your best friends? Because, when they bore you, you can shut them up without giving offense.

Why, when you are out in a boat, should you never be surprised by a sudden squall? Because, if you go for a sale, you may expect to be sold.

Why is no country free? Because anybody is liable to be sold by auction whom it is possible for the auctioneer to take in.

Why, if a man has a gallery of paintings, may you pick his pockets? Because he has picked yours (pictures).

Why are pipes all humbugs? Because the best of them are but meer-shams.

Where can you find every word of your last interesting conversation with Miss ———

all written down, word for word? In the dictionary.

What is that which a cat has but no other animal? Kittens.

Why is an egg like a colt? Because it isn't fit for use until it's broken.

How is it guns can kick when they have no legs? They kick with their breeches.

Why is a sporting clergyman like a soldier who runs from battle? Because he departs from his sphere of action.

When is a soldier charitable? When he presents arms.

Why are cowardly soldiers like tallow candles? Because when they're exposed to the fire they run.

When may an army be said to be totally destroyed? When the soldiers are all in quarters.

Why is a defeated army like wool? Because it's worsted.

What sort of men are most aboveboard in their movements? Chessmen.

Why should good-natured people never

go to small dancing parties? Because hops produce great bitterness.

What is tantalizing? Giving invitations only to teas.

Why is flirting like plate-powder? Because it brightens the spoons.

What is a kiss? A receipt given you by a lady on paying your addresses.

When are kisses sweetest? When siruptitiously (surreptitiously) obtained.

Why are two young ladies kissing each other an emblem of Christianity? Because they are doing unto each other as they would men should do unto them.

Why is confessing to a father confessor like killing bees? Because you un-buzz-'em (unbosom).

When does a leopard change his spots? When he moves from one spot to another.

When an old woman in a scarlet cloak was crossing a field in which a goat was browsing, what took place? The goat turned to butter (butt her), and the old woman into a scarlet runner.

What is the most wonderful animal in the farmyard? A pig, for he is killed and then cured.

Why is an elephant's head different from every other head? Because if you cut his head off his body you do not take it from the trunk.

Which has most legs, a cow or no cow? No cow has eight legs.

What is the difference between the cradle and the grave? The one is for the first born, the other for the last bourn.

Why must a Yankee speculator be very subject to water on the brain? Because he always has an ocean (a notion) in his head.

What trees has fire no effect upon? Ashes, as when burned, they are ashes still.

If a tree were to break the panes of a window, what would they say? Tree, mend us (tremendous).

When is a charade like a fir-tree? When you get a deal bored from its length.

Why is a jeweler like a screeching singer? Because he pierces the ears.

Why is an old man's head like a song executed by an indifferent singer? Because it is often terribly bawled (bald).

Why is a piano like an onion? Because it's mell-odious (melodious).

What sort of medicine is most like a sick monkey? A pill (ape-ill).

When is a girl like a mirror? When she's a good-looking (g)lass.

What is the difference between some women and their looking-glasses? They talk without reflecting, and the mirrors reflect without talking.

What is the best way to prevent water coming into your house? Do not pay your water rates.

What do ladies look for when they go to church? The hymns (hims).

When may a man's coat-pocket be empty and yet have something in it? When it has a hole in it.

What is the difference between a sweep and a man in mourning? One is blacked with soot, and the other is suited with black.

What is the difference between killed soldiers and repaired garments? The former are dead men, the latter are mended (men dead).

Why does a salmon die before it lives? Because its existence is ova before it comes to life.

When is a schoolboy like a postage stamp? When he is licked and put in the corner to make him stick to his letters.

What is the difference between an engine-driver and a schoolmaster? One minds the train, the other trains the mind.

When is a member of Congress ferocious? When he inserts his claws (clause) into the Bill of another member.

What is the best description of "rapid consumption"? Bolting one's food.

Why does a fox-hound wag his tail? Because he is stronger than his tail, otherwise his tail would wag him.

Why is a gooseberry tart like a bad coin? Because it's not currant (current).

When is a blow from a lady welcome? When she strikes you agreeably.

When you give a lady a lock of your hair, what else does she receive from you at the same time? A key to your feelings.

Why is a pretty girl like a locomotive engine? Because she sends off the sparks, transports the mails, has a train following her, and passes over the plain.

What part of speech is kissing? A conjunction.

Why are there more marriages in winter than in summer? Because the men seek comforters, and the ladies seek muffs.

How do the young ladies show their dislike of mustaches? By setting their faces against them.

Why are young ladies bad grammarians? Because you seldom find one who can decline Matrimony.

Where is it that all women are equally beautiful? In the dark.

Why do girls like looking at the moon? Because there's a man in it.

Why is a prosy preacher like the middle of a wheel? Because the felloes around it are tired.

Why is the rudder of a steamboat like a hangman? It has a stern duty to perform.

What is the difference between a cat and a document? One has claws at the end of its paws, and the other has pauses at the end of its clauses.

What two beaus can every lady have near at hand? El-bows.

When is a man like a cannon-ball? When he looks round.

When does the House of Representatives present one of the most ludicrous spectacles? When its ayes (eyes) are on one side, and its noes (nose) on the other.

What three acts comprise the chief business of some women's lives? Attr-act, contr-act, detr-act.

Why does a donkey eat a thistle? Because he's an ass.

What is the difference between a donkey and a postage stamp? One you lick with a stick, the other you stick with a lick.

Why shouldn't you go to church if you have a cough? Because you will be sure to disturb the *rest* of the congregation.

When is it dangerous to enter a church? When there is a canon in the reading desk, a great gun in the pulpit, and a bishop charges the congregation.

When is a rushlight like a tombstone? When it is put up for a *late* husband.

Why are women like churches? Because there is no living without one; because there is many a-spire to them; and because they are objects of adoration.

Why is your thumb, when putting on a glove, like eternity? Because it's ever-last-in' (everlasting).

Why are kisses like creation? They are made of nothing, yet are very good.

Why is a ragged beggar like a clergyman near the end of his sermon? He's tor'd his clothes.

Why is a greenback more desirable than gold? When you put it in your pocket you double it and when you take it out you find it in creases.

Why is it dangerous to walk out in the spring? The grass is full of blades, the trees are shooting, every flower has a pistil, and the bull rushes out.

What is that which, although only four inches long and three inches wide, contains a solid foot? A shoe.

What is the difference between a physician and a magician? One is a cupper, the other a sorcerer.

What becomes of all the pins? They fall to the earth, and become terra-pins.

Why is a belle like a locomotive? She transports the mails.

Why is a Freshman like a telescope? He is easily drawn out, seen through, and shut up.

Why is a flea like a long winter? It makes a backward spring.

What is the smallest room in the world? The mush-room.

What is the largest room in the world? Room for improvement.

What is that which is above all human imperfections, and yet shelters the weakest and most depraved, as well as the best of men? A hat.

Why does a man permit himself to be hen-pecked? Because he's chicken-hearted.

Why would a compliment from a chicken be an insult? Because it would be in fowl language.

Why is an aristocratic seminary for young ladies like a flower garden? Because it's a place of haughty culture (horticulture).

Why are deaf people like India shawls? Because you can't make them here (hear).

What is that which belongs to yourself, yet is used by every one more than yourself? Your name.

What tongue is that which frequently hurts and grieves you, and yet does not speak a word? The tongue of your shoe.

When may a man be said to be personally involved? When he is wrapped up in himself.

What is most like a horse's foot? A mare's.

Why is a horse an anomaly in the hunting-field? Because the better tempered he is the easier he takes a fence (offense).

What is a dogma? An opinion laid down with a snarl.

Why is a turnpike like a dead dog's tail? Because it stops a waggin'.

When are handcuffs like knapsacks? When made for two-wrists (tourists).

What is the difference between a butterfly and a volcano? In one the lava comes out of the crater, in the other the "crater" comes out of the larva.

Why is a man riding swiftly up hill like one who presents a young lady with a young dog? He gives a gallop up (gal a pup).

Why is a love of the ocean like curiosity? It has sent many a boy to sea (see).

What is the best way to double a flock of sheep? Fold them.

Why are mortgages like burglars? They secure (seek your) money.

Why is a woman's thought like the telegraph? It is so much quicker than the mail (male) intelligence.

If you lose a dollar to-day, why would it be a good plan to lose another to-morrow? So as to make your loss a-gain.

What constitutes a weighty discourse?

First to ann-*ounce* a text, then to ex-*pound* it.

What is disgusting to all but those who swallow it? Flattery.

Why is a lawyer like an honest man? He is a man of deeds as well as of words.

Why does a young man study law? To get on.

Why does he continue in the profession? To get honor.

Why does he leave the profession? To get honest.

What is the difference between fog and a falling star? One is a mist on earth, the other is missed in heaven.

Why is the present moment like skim-milk? It's scum (come).

Why is a four-quart measure like a side-saddle? They both hold a gal(l)on.

How can you shoot one hundred and twenty hares at one shot? Fire at a wig.

Name that which, with only one eye put out, has but a nose left. No*i*se.

Why are laundresses good navigators?

Because they are always crossing the line, and going from pole to pole.

What is that which if you name it even you break it? Silence.

What is that which you can keep even after giving it to somebody else? Your word.

What is that which the dead and the living do at the same time? Go round with the world.

What snuff-taker is that whose box gets fuller the more pinches he takes? The snuffers.

Why are your nose and chin constantly at variance? Because words are continually passing between them.

What is the smallest bridge in the world? The bridge of your nose.

Why is a Jew in a fever like the famous Koh-i-noor diamond? Because he's a Jew-ill.

Why is an undutiful son like one born deaf? Because your voice is lost upon him.

What is that which is put on the table

and cut, but never eaten? A pack of cards.

What fashionable game do frogs play at—besides leap-frog? Croaky (croquet).

What question is that to which you positively must answer yes? What does y-e-s spell?

What would a pig do if he wished to build himself a habitation? Tie a knot in his tail, and call it a pig's-tie (pig's sty).

If the before-mentioned porker wished to demolish the pig's sty he had built, what quotation would he make? "I could a tail (tale) unfold."

What is that which is white, black, and red all over, which shows some people to be green, and makes others look black and blue? A newspaper.

Why is a newspaper like an army? Because it has leaders, columns, and reviews.

What part of a lady's face in January is like a celebrated fur? Chin-chilly (chinchilla).

Why are suicides invariably successful people in the world? Because they always manage to accomplish their own ends.

Where is the cheapest place to buy poultry? At the State Bath House, where you can get a duck for a dime.

Why are the "blue devils" like muffins? Because they are both fancy bred (bread).

What makes more noise than a pig in a sty? Two pigs.

When would a farmer have the best opportunity for overlooking his pigs? When he has a sty in his eye.

What is lengthened by being cut at both ends? A ditch.

Why does a nobleman's title sometimes become extinct? Because, though the king can make a man appear (a peer), he can't make him apparent (a parent).

What gives a cold, cures a cold, and pays the doctor? A draft.

What is the worst kind of fare for a man to live on? Warfare.

Of what color are the winds and waves in a storm? The winds blew (blue) and the waters rose.

How does a ray of light get through a prism? It hews (hues) its way.

What would a bear want if he should get into a dry-goods store? Muslin (muzzling).

When does English butter become Irish butter? When it is made into little *Pats*.

Which is the most ancient of trees? The elder tree.

Which are the most seasonable clothes? Pepper and salt.

Why are lawyers and doctors safe people by whom to take example? Because they practice their professions.

Why is a fiddle like a man who gives money to make up a quarrel? Because it is for a-tone-ment.

Why is a good pun like a good cat? Because it requires pause (paws).

Why is a Jew's harp like a good dinner? Because it makes a man's mouth water.

Why is there a bad audience at the play-house when the pit is full? Because it is a pitiful house.

Why is a fortified town like a pudding? Because it's often batter'd.

Why does a tallow chandler live better

than another man? Because he lives on the fat of the land.

Why is a water lily like a whale? Because it comes to the surface to blow.

Why is a resolution like a looking glass? Because it is so easily broken.

Why can you never tell real hysterics from sham ones? Because in either case it is a feint (faint).

When may ladies who are enjoying themselves be said to look wretched? When at the opera, as then they are in tiers.

When is a bonnet not a bonnet? When it becomes a pretty woman.

Why is a vine like a soldier? Because it is 'listed, trained, has tendrils, and then shoots.

Why is a miserly uncle with whom you have quarreled like a person with a short memory? Because he is ever for-getting, and never for-giving.

Why are worn-out clothes like children without parents? Because they are left off'uns (orphans).

What is the difference between a milkmaid and a swallow? One skims the milk, the other the water.

Why is a very demure young lady like a tugboat? Because she pays no attention to the swells that follow her.

What smells most in a chemist's shop? The nose.

Who is your greatest friend? Your nose, because it will run for you till it drops.

Which travels faster, heat or cold? Heat, because you can easily catch cold.

What did the muffin say to the toasting fork? You're too pointed.

I am forever, yet was never. Eternity.

Which eat more grass, black sheep or white? White, because there are more of them.

Why is a very amusing man like a very bad shot? Because he keeps the game alive.

What is the height of folly? Spending your last shilling on a purse.

In what sort of family does the seventh night of the week come on the sixth? In that sort of family where Saturday is a bath night (is Sabbath night).

Why are clouds like coachmen? Because they hold the reins (rains).

On what supposition could a pocket handkerchief be used to build a house? If it became-brick (be cambric).

Why did the young lady return the dumb waiter? Because it didn't answer.

Why is a schoolboy being flogged like your eye? Because he's a pupil under the lash.

Why does a blow leave a blue mark? Because blow, when perfect, makes blew.

When has a man brown hands? When he's tand-'em driving.

Why is the leading horse in a wagon-team like the acceptor of a bill? Because he's the end horse, sir (endorser).

Why is a man marrying a second time like *sal volatile?* Because it's re-wiving.

When may a lady be absolutely pronounced to be quite past recovery? When she is speechless, and can only chatter with her teeth.

Why are ladies' eyes like persons separated by the Atlantic Ocean? Because, although they may correspond, they never meet.

What two ages often prove illusory? Mir-age and marri-age.

State the difference between a grocer selling a pound of sugar, and an apothecary's boy with a pestle and mortar. One weighs a pound, the other pounds away.

Why is gritty coffee like the Subway? It may be considered underground.

When can an Irish servant answer two questions at the same time? When she is asked, "What's o'clock, and where's the cold chicken?" if she replies, "Sure, it's ate."

Why would an owl be offended at your calling him a pheasant? Because you would be making game of him.

Why can a fish never be in the dark? Because of his parraffins (pair o' fins).

When is a candle like an ill-conditioned, quarrelsome man? When it is put out before it has had time to flare up and blaze away.

Why is love like a candle? Because the longer it burns the less it becomes.

What is the difference between a tight boot and an oak tree? One makes acorns, the other makes corns ache.

Why does the east wind never blow straight? Because it blows oblique (blows so bleak).

What is the difference between a *première danseuse* and a duck? One goes quick on her beautiful legs, the other goes "quack" on her beautiful eggs.

What is the difference between a French pastry-cook and a billsticker? One puffs up paste, the other pastes up puffs.

Why is it vulgar to sing and play by yourself? Because it is so-lo.

When is a young lady like an acrobat? When she shows her sleight of hand by refusing you.

Why is one stall of a two-stall stable like a pretty girl? Because it is seldom let alone.

Why is the root of the tongue like a dejected man? Because it is down in the mouth.

What part of one's head is fit to eat? An ear o' rye (awry).

Why cannot you make a venison pasty of buck venison? Because the pasty must be made of dough (doe).

Why ought venison to be only half-cooked? Because what is done, cannot be helped.

Why do sailors working in brigs make bad servants? Because it is impossible for a man to serve two mast-ers well.

Why are plagiarists like seashore lodging-house keepers with newly married couples? Because they are accustomed to sea-side dears (seize ideas), and to make the most out of them that is possible.

What is Majesty deprived of its externals? A jest (M-ajest-y).

Why is a cracker like death? Because it is a debt o' natur' (detonator).

What is the greatest instance of cannibalism on record? When a rash man ate a rasher.

What tree bears the most fruit to market? The axle-tree.

How is it that trees can put on new dresses without "opening their trunks"? Because they leave out their summer clothing.

What is the difference between a potato and a soldier? One shoots from the eye, the other from the shoulder.

What is the difference between a beehive and a diseased potato? None at all; one is a bee-holder (beholder), the other a speck'd tatur (spectator).

What is the difference between a piece of honeycomb and a black eye? One is produced by a laboring bee, the other by a belaboring.

Why are country girls' cheeks like well-printed cottons? Because they are warranted to wash—and keep color.

Why are volunteers like old maids? Because they are always ready, but never wanted.

Why would young ladies make good volunteers? Because they are accustomed to bare arms.

What is the difference between love and war? One breaks hearts, the other heads.

What is the difference between a volunteer and an omelet? The difference is that one is equipped to go forth, the other is egg whipped to go froth.

Why is a black man necessarily a conjurer? Because he is a negro-man-sir (necromancer).

What is that which every one frequently holds yet rarely touches? His tongue.

What is a good way to make money fast? Put it in a safety deposit box.

Why is one who uses hair dye like a suicide? Because he dies by his own hand.

Why are frames put about tomato plants? To make the tomato ketchup (catch up).

Why should wire be used to train string beans? So that they may not be too stringy.

Why is a proposal like the first conviction for drunkenness? Because it is a short sentence which generally leads to a long one.

What kind of a pen does the plagiarist use? Steel.

If an uncle's sister is not your aunt, what relation does she bear to you? **Your mother.**

Of what profession is every child? A player.

Why is Troy weight like an unconscientious person? Because it has no scruples.

Which is heavier, the half or the full moon? The half, because the full moon is as light again.

Why must a fisherman be very wealthy? Because his is all net profit.

When is a boat like a heap of snow? When it is a-drift.

What 'bus has found room for the greatest number of people? Colum-bus.

Why is an alligator the most deceitful of animals? Because he shows an open countenance in the act of taking you in.

When may a man be said to be really over head and ears in debt? **When he hasn't paid for his wig.**

What is the difference between the Prince of Wales, an orphan, a bald-headed man, and a gorilla? The first is an heir apparent, the second has ne'er a parent, the third has no hair apparent, and the fourth has a hairy parent.

When does a son not take after his father? When his father leaves him nothing to take.

Why are poor relations like fits of the gout? Because the oftener they come the longer they stay.

Why is the game of Blindman's Buff like sympathy? Because it is a fellow feeling for another.

When could you eat a lady's hand? When it is a warm muff in.

Just state the difference between an auction and sea-sickness. One is a sale of effects, the other the effects of a sail.

Why does a man who has been all his life a woodcutter, never come home to dinner? Because he's not only bred (bread) there, but he's always a chop in (a-choppin') the wood.

What is the difference between a soldier and a fisherman? One bayonets, the other nets a bay.

What musical instrument invites you to fish? Cast-a-net (castanet).

What is the difference between a fisherman and a lazy schoolboy? One baits his hook, the other hates his book.

What words may be pronounced quicker and shorter by adding syllables to them? Quick and short.

What is the worth of a woman? Double you, O man (w-o-man).

Why is a kiss like a rumor? Because it goes from mouth to mouth.

What shape is a kiss? A-lip-tickle (elliptical).

What becomes every woman? A blush.

Why are three couples going to be married like penny trumpets? Because they go two-two-two.

What is that which fastens two people together, yet touches only one? The wedding-ring.

What is a ring? A hole with a rim around it.

What grows bigger the more you contract it? Debt.

Why is a spendthrift, with regard to his fortune, like the water in a filter? Because he soon runs through it, and leaves many matters behind to settle.

Why are birds melancholy in the morning? Because their little bills are all over dew (overdue).

What is the difference between a last will and testament and a man who has eaten as much as he can? One is signed and dated, and the other is dined and sated.

What is the greatest feat, in the eating way, ever known? That recorded of a man who commenced by bolting a door, after which he threw up a window, and then sat down and swallowed a whole story.

How should love come to the door? With a ring.

If a mercenary man were to ask a girl to marry, what flower would he name? Any money (anemone).

When may two people be said to be half-witted? When there is an understanding between them.

Why is the science of self-defense like low tide? It develops the muscles.

Why should a teetotaler never take a wife? He will not sup-porter (support her).

Why should free seats at church be abolished? They make people good for nothing.

What relation is the door-mat to the threshold? A step-father (farther).

When is love deformed? When it is all on one side.

Where have you the most extended view? In a hop-garden, for then you see from pole to pole.

What burns to keep a secret? Sealing wax.

Plant the setting sun, and what will come up? The morning glory.

Why is a dog with a lame leg like a boy ciphering? He puts down three and carries one,

Why are eyes like stage-horses? They are always under the lash.

What is the brightest idea of the day? Your eye, dear.

Why are ladies bathing like a Yankee drink? They are 'lasses in water.

Of what color is grass under snow? Invisible green.

What is the hardest conundrum? Life, because we all have to give it up.

What is that which is often given you, which you never have, yet which you often give up? A conundrum.

What kin is that child to his own father who is not his own father's son? His daughter.

If Dick's father is Tom's son, what relation is Dick to Tom? Tom is his grandfather.

When does a man sneeze three times? When he cannot help it.

Why does a piebald pony never pay toll? Because his master pays it for him.

HANDBOOK OF CONUNDRUMS

When may a man be said to have four hands? When he doubles his fists.

What goes over the water and under the water, but never touches the water? A woman crossing a bridge with a pail of water on her head.

How many peas in a pint? One.

When is a soldier like a watch? When he is on guard.

How is a poultry dealer compelled to earn his living? By fowl means.

Why is a butcher's cart like his top boots? Because he carries his calves there.

Why does a cat rest better in summer? Because summer brings a cat-a-pillow (caterpillar).

What is it that every man overlooks? His nose.

Why should potatoes grow better than any other vegetable? Because they have eyes to see what they are doing.

What were the last words of the bugler who was gored by the bull? "Blow the horn

Why are lawyers like shears? Because they do not cut each other, but only what comes between them.

What have feet and walk not? Stoves.

What have eyes and see not? Potatoes.

What have noses but smell not? Teapots.

What have hands but work not? Clocks.

What have mouths but eat not? Rivers.

What have ears but hear not? Cornstalks.

What have tongues but talk not? Wagons.

Why do we all go to bed? Because the bed will not come to us.

What is higher and handsomer when the head is off? A pillow.

What is the best thing to make in a hurry? Haste.

Why do dentists make good politicians? Because they have a great pull.

If a tailor and a goose are on the top of a monument, what is the quickest way for the tailor to get down? Pluck the goose.

If I walk into a room full of people and place a new penny upon the table in full view of the company, what does the coin do? It looks round.

Why is a mouse like hay? Because the cat'll eat it (cattle).

Why is a madman equal to two men? Because he is one beside himself.

Which member of Congress wears the largest hat? The one who has the largest head.

When does a pig become landed property? When he is turned into a meadow.

What is the difference between a cow and a rickety chair? One gives milk and the other gives whey (way).

What flower most resembles a bull's mouth? The cowslip.

When is a lady deformed? When mending stockings; because she then has her hands where her feet ought to be.

Why is the proprietor of a balloon like a phantom? Because he's an airy-nought (aëronaut).

Why do little birds in their nests agree? For fear of falling out.

Why is the flight of an eagle a most unpleasant sight to witness? Because it's an eye-sore ('igh soar).

What impermeable fabric is a sparrow like? Gutter percher (gutta percha).

Which of the feathered tribe can lift the heaviest weights? The crane.

Why does the rope dancer invariably have to repeat his performances? Because they are always on cord (encored).

What is the difference between a widow and a window? Little if n-y; for the transparents griefs of the one, like the panes of the other, are removed in course of re-pairing; and the latter is for mankind to look out of, while the former looks out for mankind.

When may a loaf of bread be said to be inhabited? When it has a little Indian in it.

What part of a fish weighs most? The scales.

What is that which works when it plays and plays when it works? A fountain.

Why is divinity the easiest of the three learned professions? Because it is easier to preach than to practice.

Why are sailors bad horsemen? Because they ride on the main (mane).

Why is a sword belt like a cow upon a common? Because it goes round the waste (waist).

Why is a thief like a knocker? Because they are tied up to prevent disturbance.

What's the difference between a bee and a donkey? One gets all the honey, and the other all the whacks (wax).

Why is sealing wax like a rifleman? Because it's often under arms.

Why are cripples and beggars similar to shepherds and fishermen? Because they live by hook and by crook.

What is that which has four legs and flies in the air? Two canary birds.

What is the only pain of which every one makes light? A window pane.

Why is a smith a dangerous companion? Because he deals in forgery.

Why are coals like poor laboring men? Because they feed the great.

Why is an honest friend like orange chips? Because he's candid.

Why is a peach-stone like a regiment? Because it has a colonel (kernel).

Why is a playhouse like a punch bowl? Because it is best when full.

What is the principal part of a horse? The mane (main) part.

Why is a candle like an atheist? Because it's wicked.

Why is a dog like a tree? Because they both produce a bark.

What barrel is best fitted for a soldier's helmet? A cask (casque).

Why is it no offense to conspire in the evening? What is treasonable is reasonable after *t*.

Why is a corpse like a man with a cold? Because he is in a-coughing.

Why is a fiddler like a man in amaze? Because he's at a stand.

What part of a fish is like the end of a book? The fin-is.

What language should a linguist end with? The Finnish.

What sea is most traveled by clever intellectual people? Brilliancy.

What is the difference between a butcher and a flirt? One kills to dress, the other dresses to kill.

Why is marriage with a deceased wife's sister like the wedding of two fish? Because it's a-finny-tie (affinity).

A man bought two fishes, but on taking them home found he had three; how was this? He had two—and one smelt.

If the poker, shovel, and tongs cost five dollars, what would a ton of coal come to? To ashes.

Why is a blacksmith the most dissatisfied of all mechanics? Because he's always on the strike for wages.

Why is selling off bankrupt goods like preparing a dish of soup? Because it is a liquidation of stock.

Why is a wide-awake so called? Because it never had a nap, and never wants one.

What is the difference between a young lady and a wide-awake hat? One has feeling, the other is felt.

What is worse than raining cats and dogs? Hailing street cars.

What is the oldest lunatic on record? Time out of mind.

How can you make one pound of green tea go as far as five pounds of black? Buy the above quantities in Boston, and send them down to New York.

Why is a patent safety Hansom cab a dangerous carriage to drive in? Because the cabman always drives over your head.

Why is whispering in company like a forged bank note? Because it is uttered but not allowed.

Which constellation resembles an empty fireplace? The Great Bear.

What is the last remedy for a smoky chimney. Putting the fire out.

Why is a clever wit like a chemist? Because he has many a good retort.

Why is a bankrupt husband an ardent lover? Because his is unremitting affection.

What is the difference between a spendthrift and a feather bed? One is hard up and the other soft down.

What comes after cheese? Mouse.

Why is a mouse entering a mouse trap like a diplomat arguing his policy? Because each has a well-defined end in view.

When may a man be said to breakfast before he gets up? When he takes a roll in bed.

When are volunteers not volunteers? When they are mustered (mustard).

Which is the merriest sauce? Caper sauce.

Why is a cat going up three pairs of stairs like a high hill? Because she's a-mounting (a mountain).

Why is a lead pencil like a perverse child? Because it never does write (right) by itself.

Why are wooden ships, as compared with ironclads, of the female sex? Because they are the weaker vessels.

At what time of life may a man be said to belong to the vegetable kingdom? When long experience has made him sage.

When is a sailor not a sailor? When he is aloft.

What wild animals may be correctly shut up in one enclosure? Twelve ounces in one pound.

What makes a pair of boots? Two boots.

What tree is of the greatest importance in history? The date.

Why is the superintendent of a children's play-ground like a stranded vessel? Because he runs a-ground.

Why is the road-bed laborer on a railroad like a hunted bear in the mountains? Because he makes tracks for his life.

Why is the engineer of a train like an aëronaut? Because he frequently slows down.

Why is it impossible that there should be a best horse on a race course? Because there is always a bettor.

When may a ship be said to be in love? When she wishes for a mate.

What is that which has never been felt, seen, or heard,—never existed, and still has a name? Nothing.

Why is a congreve-box without matches superior to all other boxes? Because it is matchless.

Why is a postman in danger of losing his way? Because he is guided by the directions of strangers.

What is that which comes with a coach, goes with a coach, is of no use to the coach, and yet the coach cannot go without it? Noise.

Why is a missionary like a pig roasting on a spit? Because he goes around doing good.

Why are hogs more intelligent than humans? Because they nose (knows) everything.

What makes a pet dog wag his tail when he sees his master? Because he's got one to wag.

What other edifice does a man sometimes

carry about with him besides a sty in his eye? A castle in the (h)air.

When is a fast young man nearest heaven? When on a lark.

When is a cigar like a shoulder of pork? When it's smoked.

When is a man most likely to get floored (flawed)? When he's up late (a plate), and so runs a chance of becoming cracked.

What are the features of the cannon? Cannon-mouth, canon-ize, and cannon-eers.

Who always sits with his hat on before the queen? Her coachman.

Why is a pig in the drawing-room like a house on fire? Because the sooner it is put out the better.

When is a river not a river? When it is eye water (high water).

What trade never turns to the left? A wheelwright.

What trade is more than full? Fuller.

Why is electricity like the police when they are wanted? Because it is an invisible force.

When is a borough like a ship? When it is under canvass.

Why are guns like trees? People plant them and they shoot.

How does a boy look if you hurt him? It makes him yell O! (yellow).

What part of your ear would be the most essential for a martial band? The drum.

What is it that stands aloft, and regulates our daily movements, yet feels no interest in our concerns; directs us when to go, and when to come; yet cares not whether we attend or not; still, thus indifferent to our fate, often strikes a heavy blow to urge us on, and we feel no resentment when the reproof is given? A clock.

Why is the dove a very cautious little dear? Because he minds his peas and coos.

When is a baby like a breakfast cup? When it's a tea thing (teething).

Why is a chicken served to a minister like a theological student? Because it is about to enter the ministry.

What animal keeps the best time? A watch dog.

When is a young lady's cheek not a cheek? When it is a little pale (pail).

When is a nose not a nose? When it is a little reddish (radish).

What sort of a face does the auctioneer like best? One that is for-bidding.

When is a straight field not a straight field? When it is a rye field (a wry).

What is it that walks with its head downward? A nail in a shoe.

Why are the hours from one to twelve like good Christians? Because they are always on the watch.

Why is a hen walking across the road like a conspiracy? Because it is a foul proceeding.

What sort of sympathy would you rather be without? You don't want to be pitted by the small-pox.

What is that which we often return but never borrow? Thanks.

What animals are always seen at a funeral? Black kids.

What did the pistol ball say to the

wounded duelist? "I hope I give satisfaction."

Why is horse racing a necessity? Because it is a matter of course.

What is a young lady who refuses you? Two no-ing by half.

Why is a note of hand like a rosebud? Because it is matured by falling due (dew).

What games do the waves play at? At pitch and toss.

What fish is most valued by a loving wife? Her-ring.

Why is a solar eclipse like a woman whipping her boy? Because it's a hiding of the son (sun).

When does a man's hair resemble a packing box? When it stands on end.

Why is a woman who tries to drive a balky horse like a successful actress? Because she's the leading lady.

Why is a mad bull an animal of convivial disposition? Because he offers a horn to every one he meets.

When is silence likely to get wet? When it reigns.

How do you make a Maltese cross? Pull its tail.

What is a waste (waist) of time? The middle of an hour glass.

Who is the most popular preacher? Jack in the pulpit. Why? Because he is silent.

Why is a muddy road a guardian of the public safety? Because it reduces the speed of autos.

Why does a student never lead a sedentary life? Because he's always pursuing his studies.

Why are bishops like superannuated washerwomen? Because they wear lawn dresses (were laundresses).

Why can no clergyman have a wooden leg? Because, although a chaplain may be a plain chap, a parson can't be a lame un (layman).

If thirty-two degrees is freezing point, what is squeezing point? Two in the shade.

What is that which becomes too young the longer it exists? A portrait.

What is that which we often catch yet never see? A passing remark.

What is the geometrical form of an escaped parrot? A polygon (polly gone).

Why is a lamp like a house? Because it has a chimney.

Why is the wall going to decay? Because you can see its molding.

How does a tipsy man generally look? Dizzy-pated.

At what age should a man marry? At the parsonage.

Why is a committee of inquiry like a cannon? It makes a report.

What is the most popular paper at a summer resort? Flypaper.

What coat is finished without buttons and put on wet? A coat of paint.

Why do you think that a judge of the criminal court is looked upon with contempt? Because every day the worst of scoundrels are set before him.

Why is a book like a king? It has many pages.

What roof never keeps out the wet? The roof of the mouth.

What fruit is on a cent? A date.

Why are good women like ivy? Because the greater the ruin, the closer they cling.

Why are bad women like ivy? Because the closer they cling the greater the ruin.

Echoes

What must be done to conduct a newspaper right? Write.

What is necessary to a farmer to assist him? System.

What would give a blind man the greatest delight? Light.

What is the best advice to give a justice of the peace? Peace.

Who commit the greatest abominations? Nations.

Who is the greatest terrifier? Fire.

What made the tart tart? Because she didn't want the baker to bake her.

CHAPTER X

Charades, Stories, and Contests

My first makes company,
My second shuns company,
My third assembles company,
My whole puzzles company.
                    Co-nun-drum.

My first is a reflection, my second not so much, and my whole none at all. Thoughtless.

I lived upon my own substance and died when I had devoured myself. A candle.

I have hands, but no fingers; no bed, but a tick. A clock.

You can hang me on the wall, but if you take me down, you cannot hang me up again. Wall paper.

In my first my second sat, my third and fourth I ate. In-sat-i-ate.

May my first never be lost in my second,
To prevent me from enjoying my whole.
      Friendship.

My first I do, and my second—when I say you are my whole—I do not. Love-lie (Lovely).

My first is a prop, my second also is a prop, and my whole is a prop as well. Footstool.

Wipe my face, and I'm everybody; scratch my back, and I'm nobody. A mirror.

By well employing my second you will never regret my first, and you will the more thoroughly enjoy my whole. Past-time.

When you stole my first, I lost my second, and you are the only person to give me my whole. Hearts-ease.

Why is the emblem of America more lasting than that of France, England, Ireland, or Scotland?

 The lily may fade, and its leaves decay,
  The rose from its stem may sever;
 Shamrock and thistle may pass away,
  But the stars shall shine for ever.

Read   see   that   me   but   not   my   got
 Up   shall   I   love   if   me   love for-
And   you   love you   that love for   be
Down   and   you   if   you   do   you shall
   Read up and down and you shall see.

        Can you tell me why
        A hypocrite's eye
        Can better descry
        Than you or I
        On how many toes
        A pussy-cat goes?

        A man of deceit
        Can best count-er-feit;
        And so, I suppose,
        Can best count her toes.

My first, though 'tis dirty, 's a thing to a door;
My second is made into cakes and a bun;
My third is, believe me, by none thought a bore;
My whole we have frequently been led to believe by many authors of the United States is very often indeed called one.
Mat-ry(e)-money.

Why is a cross old bachelor like the pre-

ceding conundrum? Because he's averse to matrimony.

By equal division, I know I am right;
The half of thirteen you'll find to be eight.

$$XIII, \frac{VIII}{\Lambda III}, VIII$$

I came to a field and couldn't get through it;
So I went to school and learned how to do it.
> Fence.

Legs have I got, but seldom walk,
I backbite all, yet never talk.
> A flea.

I am a good state, there can be no doubt of it;
But those who are in, entirely are out of it.
> Sane; insane.

Formed long ago, yet made to-day,
 I'm most employed while others sleep;
What none would like to give away,
 Yet no one likes to keep.
> Bed.

My first of anything is half,
 My second is complete;
And so remains until once more
 My first and second meet.
> Semi-circle.

Pray tell me, ladies, if you can,
Who is that highly favored man,
Who, though he has married many a wife,
May still live single all his life?
A clergyman.

Great numbers do our use despise,
　　But yet, at last they find,
Without our help in many things,
　　They might as well be blind.
Spectacles.

My love for you will never know
　　My first, nor yet my second;
'Tis like your wit and beauty, so
　　My whole 'twill aye be reckoned.
End-less.

As I was going through a field of wheat,
I found something good to eat;
It wasn't fish or flesh or bone;
I kept it till it ran alone.
An egg.

There's a word composed of three letters alone
　　Which reads backwards and forwards the same,
It expresses the sentiments warm from the heart,

And to beauty lays principal claim.
Eye.

We travel much, yet pris'ners are,
  And close confined to boot;
We with the swiftest horse keep pace,
  Yet always go on foot.
A pair of spurs.

My first doth affliction denote,
  Which my second is destined to feel;
But my whole is the sure antidote
  That affliction to soothe and to heal.
Wo-man.

Those who take me improve, be their task what it may,
Those who have me are sorrowful through the long day;
I am hated alike by the foolish and wise,
Yet without me none ever to eminence rise.
Pains.

Your initials begin with an A,
You've an A at the end of your name,
The whole of your name is an A,
And it's backwards and forwards the same.
Anna.

Ever running on my race,
Never staying at one place,

Through the world I make my tour,
Everywhere at the same hour.
If you please to spell my name,
Reversed or forward it's the same.
      Noon.

You name me once, and I am famed
 For deeds of noble daring;
You name me twice, and I am found
 In savage customs sharing.
      Tar-tar.

What is that which lives in winter, dies in summer, and grows with its root upwards? An icicle.

Water soft is my first, water hard is my second,
Sticks made of my whole are by many sweet reckon'd.
     Liquor-ice (licorice).

From a number that's odd cut off the head,
 It then will even be.
Its tail, I pray, next take away,
 Your mother then you'll see.
     Seven—even—Eve.

My first is of illustrious line,
Of beauteous form and face divine;
Which when my second does assail,

Both form and beauty then do fail;
My whole an arduous task to do
With wives who hoity-toity ways pursue.
                    Man-age.

A stranger comes from foreign shores,
   Perchance to seek relief;
Curtail him, and you find his tale
   Unworthy of belief;
Curtailed again, you recognize
   An old Egyptian chief.
                    Alien—a lie—Ali.

An ugly little fellow, that some might call a pet,
Was easily transmuted to a parson when he ate;
And when he set off running, an Irishman was he;
Then took to wildly raving, and hung upon a tree.
            Cur, cur-ate, Cur-ran, cur-rant.

Ere Adam was, my early days began;
I ape each creature, and resemble man;
I gently creep o'er tops of tender grass,
Nor leave the least impression where I pass;
Touch me you may, but I can ne'er be felt,
Nor ever yet was tasted, heard, or smelt,
Yet seen each day; if not, be sure at night

You'll quickly find me out by candlelight.
>Shadow.

'Twas whispered in Heaven, 'twas muttered in Hell,
And echo caught faintly the sound as it fell;
On the confines of earth 'twas permitted to rest,
And the depths of the ocean its presence confessed.
'Twill be found in the sphere when 'tis riven asunder,
Be seen in the lightning, and heard in the thunder.
'Twas allotted to man with his earliest breath,
Attends at his birth, and awaits him in death;
It presides o'er his happiness, honor, and health,
Is the prop of his house, and the end of his wealth.
In the whispers of conscience its voice will be found,
Nor e'en in the whirlwind of passion be drowned.
In the heaps of the miser 'tis hoarded with care,
But is sure to be lost by his prodigal heir.

'Twill not soften the heart, and though deaf to the ear,
'Twill make it acutely and instantly hear.
Without it the soldier and sailor may roam,
But woe to the wretch who expels it from home!
So in shade let it rest, like a delicate flower:
Oh, breathe on it softly, it dies in an hour!
                    The letter "H."

Stories

How do you punctuate the sentence, "I saw a five-dollar bill on the street?" Make a dash after it.

There was a carpenter who made a cupboard door; it proved too big. He cut it, and unfortunately, he cut it too little; he thereupon cut it again, and made it fit beautifully. How was this? He did not cut it enough the first time.

There are twelve birds in a covey. A hunter kills a brace, then how many remain? None, for, unless they are idiots, they fly away.

A one-eyed beggar bet a friend that he could see more with one eye than his friend could with two. How was this? Because he saw his friend's two eyes, whilst the other only saw his one.

A hunter and his dog went out hunting. The dog went not behind, went not before, nor on one side of him. Where did he go? On the other side.

Which would you rather—look a greater fool than you are, or be a greater fool than you look? (Let the person choose, then say, "That is impossible.")

Which would you rather—that a lion ate you or a tiger? Why, you would rather that the lion ate the tiger, of course.

A man stopped before the window of a trunk store; within, a large trunk was marked "$25.00," a medium-sized one "$15.00," and a small one bore the placard, "This size for $5.00." "So do I," the man said, and walked on.

A man was crossing a bridge over a small stream, and noticed a sign which read, "Don't fish here." "Do they?" he asked, and walked on.

Age Contest

What age will people reach if they live long enough? Dotage.

To what age do most people look forward? Marriage.

A necessary attribute of a soldier? Courage.

What age is required at sea? Tonnage.

What age are we forbidden to worship? Image.

What age do people get stuck on? Mucilage.

What age is neither more nor less? Average.

What is the age of profanity? Damage.

At what age will vessels ride safely? Anchorage.

What age does the infant in arms pass through? Crib-bage.

What age does the small boy enjoy? Sauce-age (sausage).

What age is the young lady most interested in? Garb-age.

What age does the child in primary school dislike? Ad(d)-age.

What age does the bride desire? Dotage.

What age is necessary for a clergyman? Parsonage.

What is the age of communication? Postage.

What age is most important to travelers? Mileage.

What is the age of slavery? Bondage.

What age is served for breakfast? Sausage.

What is the most indigestible age? Cabbage.

What age signifies the farmer? Tillage.

What age belongs to travelers? Baggage.

What age is an indication of wealth? Acreage.

What age do milliners delight in? Plumage.

What age is shared by a doctor and a lawyer? Patronage.

What age is used in turkey stuffing? (S)age.

What age do a number of people enjoy in common? Village.

Ant Contest

What is the oldest ant? Adam-ant.
What ant hires his home? Tenant.
What ant is joyful? Jubilant.
What ant is learned? Savant.
What ant is well informed? Conversant.
What ant is trustworthy? Confidant.
What ant is proud? Arrogant.
What ant sees things? Observant.
What ant is angry? Indignant.
What ant tells things? Informant.
What ant is successful? Triumphant.
What ant is an officer? Commandant.
What ant is a beggar? Mendicant.
What ant is obstinate? Defiant.
What ant is youngest? Infant.

What is the ruling ant? Dominant.
What is the wandering ant? Errant.
What ant lives in a house? Occupant.
What ant points out things? Significant.
What ant is prayerful? Supplicant.

City Contest

What city is for few people? Scarcity.
    Happy people? Felicity.
    Hypocrites? Duplicity.
    Chauffeurs? Velocity.
    Truthful people? Veracity.
    Athletes? Elasticity.
    Greedy people? Voracity.
    Wild beasts? Ferocity.
    Home lovers? Domesticity.
    Actors? Publicity.
    Reporters? Audacity.
    Wise people? Sagacity.
    Hungry people? Capacity.
    Telegraph operators? Electricity.

Crowds? Multiplicity.
Nations? Reciprocity.
Old people? Eccentricity.
Beggars? Mendicity.
Unhappy people? Infelicity.
Office-seekers? Pertinacity.

THE END

(5)

Featured Titles from Westphalia Press

Issues in Maritime Cyber Security Edited by Nicole K. Drumhiller, Fred S. Roberts, Joseph DiRenzo III and Fred S. Roberts

While there is literature about the maritime transportation system, and about cyber security, to date there is very little literature on this converging area. This pioneering book is beneficial to a variety of audiences looking at risk analysis, national security, cyber threats, or maritime policy.

The Rise of the Book Plate: An Exemplative of the Art by W. G. Bowdoin, Introduction by Henry Blackwel

Bookplates were made to denote ownership and hopefully steer the volume back to the rightful shelf if borrowed. They often contained highly stylized writing, drawings, coat of arms, badges or other images of interest to the owner.

**The Great Indian Religions
by G. T. Bettany**

G. T. (George Thomas) Bettany (1850-1891) was born and educated in England, attending Gonville and Caius College in Cambridge University, studying medicine and the natural sciences. This book is his account of Brahmanism, Hinduism, Buddhism, and Zoroastrianism

Unworkable Conservatism: Small Government, Freemarkets, and Impracticality by Max J. Skidmore

Unworkable Conservatism looks at what passes these days for "conservative" principles—small government, low taxes, minimal regulation—and demonstrates that they are not feasible under modern conditions.

A Place in the Lodge: Dr. Rob Morris, Freemasonry and the Order of the Eastern Star by Nancy Stearns Theiss PhD

Ridiculed as "petticoat masonry," critics of the Order of the Eastern Star did not deter Rob Morris' goal to establish a Masonic organization that included women as members. As Rob Morris (1818-1888) came "into the light," he donned his Masonic apron and carried the ideals of Freemasonry through a despairing time of American history.

Demand the Impossible: Essays in History as Activism
Edited by Nathan Wuertenberg and William Horne

Demand the Impossible asks scholars what they can do to help solve present-day crises. The twelve essays in this volume draw inspiration from present-day activists. They examine the role of history in shaping ongoing debates over monuments, racism, clean energy, health care, poverty, and the Democratic Party.

International or Local Ownership?: Security Sector Development in Post-Independent Kosovo
by Dr. Florian Qehaja

International or Local Ownership? contributes to the debate on the concept of local ownership in post-conflict settings, and discussions on international relations, peacebuilding, security and development studies.

The Bahai Movement: A Series of Nineteen Papers
by Charles Mason Remey

Charles Mason Remey (1874-1974) was the son of Admiral George Collier Remey and grew up in Washington DC. He studied to be an architect at Cornell (1893-1896) and the Ecole des Beaux Arts in Paris (1896-1903), where he learned about the Baha'i faith, and quickly adopted it.

Ongoing Issues in Georgian Policy and Public Administration
Edited by Bonnie Stabile and Nino Ghonghadze

Thriving democracy and representative government depend upon a well functioning civil service, rich civic life and economic success. Georgia has been considered a top performer among countries in South Eastern Europe seeking to establish themselves in the post-Soviet era.

Poverty in America: Urban and Rural Inequality and Deprivation in the 21st Century
Edited by Max J. Skidmore

Poverty in America too often goes unnoticed, and disregarded. This perhaps results from America's general level of prosperity along with a fairly widespread notion that conditions inevitably are better in the USA than elsewhere. Political rhetoric frequently enforces such an erroneous notion.

---

westphaliapress.org

www.ingramcontent.com/pod-product-compliance
Lightning Source LLC
Chambersburg PA
CBHW061319040426
42444CB00011B/2707